The Law School Admission Council (LSAC) is a nonprofit corporation that provides unique, state-of-the-art admission products and services to ease the admission process for law schools and their applicants worldwide. More than 200 law schools in the United States, Canada, and Australia are members of the Council and benefit from LSAC's services.

© 2012 by Law School Admission Council, Inc.

TABLE OF CONTENTS

INTRODUCTION TO THE LSAT

The Law School Admission Test is a half-day standardized test required for admission to all ABA-approved law schools, most Canadian law schools, and many other law schools. It consists of five 35-minute sections of multiple-choice questions. Four of the five sections contribute to the test taker's score. These sections include one Reading Comprehension section, one Analytical Reasoning section, and two Logical Reasoning sections. The unscored section, commonly referred to as the variable section, typically is used to pretest new test questions or to preequate new test forms. The placement of this section in the LSAT will vary. A 35-minute writing sample is administered at the end of the test. The writing sample is not scored by LSAC, but copies are sent to all law schools to which you apply. The score scale for the LSAT is 120 to 180.

The LSAT is designed to measure skills considered essential for success in law school: the reading and comprehension of complex texts with accuracy and insight; the organization and management of information and the ability to draw reasonable inferences from it; the ability to think critically; and the analysis and evaluation of the reasoning and arguments of others.

The LSAT provides a standard measure of acquired reading and verbal reasoning skills that law schools can use as one of several factors in assessing applicants.

For up-to-date information about LSAC's services, go to our website, LSAC.org.

SCORING

Your LSAT score is based on the number of questions you answer correctly (the raw score). There is no deduction for incorrect answers, and all questions count equally. In other words, there is no penalty for guessing.

Test Score Accuracy—Reliability and Standard Error of Measurement

Candidates perform at different levels on different occasions for reasons quite unrelated to the characteristics of a test itself. The accuracy of test scores is best described by the use of two related statistical terms: reliability and standard error of measurement.

Reliability is a measure of how consistently a test measures the skills being assessed. The higher the reliability coefficient for a test, the more certain we can be that test takers would get very similar scores if they took the test again.

LSAC reports an internal consistency measure of reliability for every test form. Reliability can vary from 0.00 to 1.00, and a test with no measurement error would have a reliability coefficient of 1.00 (never attained in practice). Reliability coefficients for past LSAT forms have ranged from .90 to .95, indicating a high degree of consistency for these tests. LSAC expects the reliability of the LSAT to continue to fall within the same range.

LSAC also reports the amount of measurement error associated with each test form, a concept known as the standard error of measurement (SEM). The SEM, which is usually about 2.6 points, indicates how close a test taker's observed score is likely to be to his or her true score. True scores are theoretical scores that would be obtained from perfectly reliable tests with no measurement error—scores never known in practice.

Score bands, or ranges of scores that contain a test taker's true score a certain percentage of the time, can be derived using the SEM. LSAT score bands are constructed by adding and subtracting the (rounded) SEM to and from an actual LSAT score (e.g., the LSAT score, plus or minus 3 points). Scores near 120 or 180 have asymmetrical bands. Score bands constructed in this manner will contain an individual's true score approximately 68 percent of the time.

Measurement error also must be taken into account when comparing LSAT scores of two test takers. It is likely that small differences in scores are due to measurement error rather than to meaningful differences in ability. The standard error of score differences provides some guidance as to the importance of differences between two scores. The standard error of score differences is approximately 1.4 times larger than the standard error of measurement for the individual scores.

Thus, a test score should be regarded as a useful but approximate measure of a test taker's abilities as measured by the test, not as an exact determination of his or her abilities. LSAC encourages law schools to examine the range of scores within the interval that probably contains the test taker's true score (e.g., the test taker's score band) rather than solely interpret the reported score alone.

Adjustments for Variation in Test Difficulty

All test forms of the LSAT reported on the same score scale are designed to measure the same abilities, but one test form may be slightly easier or more difficult than another. The scores from different test forms are made comparable through a statistical procedure known as equating. As a result of equating, a given scaled score earned on different test forms reflects the same level of ability.

Research on the LSAT

Summaries of LSAT validity studies and other LSAT research can be found in member law school libraries and at LSAC.org.

To Inquire About Test Questions

If you find what you believe to be an error or ambiguity in a test question that affects your response to the question, contact LSAC by e-mail: LSATTS@LSAC.org, or write to Law School Admission Council, Test Development Group, PO Box 40, Newtown, PA 18940-0040.

HOW THIS PREPTEST DIFFERS FROM AN ACTUAL LSAT

This PrepTest is made up of the scored sections and writing sample from the actual disclosed LSAT administered in June 2012. However, it does not contain the extra, variable section that is used to pretest new test items of one of the three multiple-choice question types. The three multiple-choice question types may be in a different order in an actual LSAT than in this PrepTest. This is because the order of these question types is intentionally varied for each administration of the test.

THE THREE LSAT MULTIPLE-CHOICE QUESTION TYPES

The multiple-choice questions that make up most of the LSAT reflect a broad range of academic disciplines and are intended to give no advantage to candidates from a particular academic background.

The five sections of the test contain three different question types. The following material presents a general discussion of the nature of each question type and some strategies that can be used in answering them.

Analytical Reasoning Questions

Analytical Reasoning questions are designed to assess the ability to consider a group of facts and rules, and, given those facts and rules, determine what could or must be true. The specific scenarios associated with these questions are usually unrelated to law, since they are intended to be accessible to a wide range of test takers. However, the skills tested parallel those involved in determining what could or must be the case given a set of regulations, the terms of a contract, or the facts of a legal case in relation to the law. In Analytical Reasoning questions, you are asked to reason deductively from a set of statements and rules or principles that describe relationships among persons, things, or events.

Analytical Reasoning questions appear in sets, with each set based on a single passage. The passage used for each set of questions describes common ordering relationships or grouping relationships, or a combination of both types of relationships. Examples include scheduling employees for work shifts, assigning instructors to class sections, ordering tasks according to priority, and distributing grants for projects.

Analytical Reasoning questions test a range of deductive reasoning skills. These include:

- Comprehending the basic structure of a set of relationships by determining a complete solution to the problem posed (for example, an acceptable seating arrangement of all six diplomats around a table)

- Reasoning with conditional ("if-then") statements and recognizing logically equivalent formulations of such statements

- Inferring what could be true or must be true from given facts and rules

- Inferring what could be true or must be true from given facts and rules together with new information in the form of an additional or substitute fact or rule

- Recognizing when two statements are logically equivalent in context by identifying a condition or rule that could replace one of the original conditions while still resulting in the same possible outcomes

Analytical Reasoning questions reflect the kinds of detailed analyses of relationships and sets of constraints that a law student must perform in legal problem solving. For example, an Analytical Reasoning passage might describe six diplomats being seated around a table, following certain rules of protocol as to who can sit where. You, the test taker, must answer questions about the logical implications of given and new information. For example, you may be asked who can sit between diplomats X and Y, or who cannot sit next to X if W sits next to Y. Similarly, if you were a student in law school, you might be asked to analyze a scenario involving a set of particular circumstances and a set of governing rules in the form of constitutional provisions, statutes, administrative codes, or prior rulings that have been upheld. You might then be asked to determine the legal options in the scenario: what is required given the scenario, what is permissible given the scenario, and what is prohibited given the scenario. Or you might be asked to develop a "theory" for the case: when faced with an incomplete set of facts about the case, you must fill in the picture based on what is implied by the facts that are known. The problem could be elaborated by the addition of new information or hypotheticals.

No formal training in logic is required to answer these questions correctly. Analytical Reasoning questions are intended to be answered using knowledge, skills, and reasoning ability generally expected of college students and graduates.

Suggested Approach

Some people may prefer to answer first those questions about a passage that seem less difficult and then those that seem more difficult. In general, it is best to finish one passage before starting on another, because much time can be lost in returning to a passage and reestablishing familiarity with its relationships. However, if you are having great difficulty on one particular set of questions and are spending too much time on them, it may be to your advantage to skip that set of questions and go on to the next passage, returning to the problematic set of questions after you have finished the other questions in the section.

Do not assume that because the conditions for a set of questions look long or complicated, the questions based on those conditions will be especially difficult.

Read the passage carefully. Careful reading and analysis are necessary to determine the exact nature of the relationships involved in an Analytical Reasoning passage. Some relationships are fixed (for example, P and R must always work on the same project). Other relationships are variable (for example, Q must be assigned to either team 1 or team 3). Some relationships that are not stated explicitly in the conditions are implied by and can be deduced from those that are stated (for example, if one condition about paintings in a display specifies that Painting K must be to the left of Painting Y, and another specifies that Painting W must be to the left of Painting K, then it can be deduced that Painting W must be to the left of Painting Y).

In reading the conditions, do not introduce unwarranted assumptions. For instance, in a set of questions establishing relationships of height and weight among the members of a team, do not assume that a person who is taller than another person must weigh more than that person. As another example, suppose a set involves ordering and a question in the set asks what must be true if both X and Y must be earlier than Z; in this case, do not assume that X must be earlier than Y merely because X is mentioned before Y. All the information needed to answer each question is provided in the passage and the question itself.

The conditions are designed to be as clear as possible. Do not interpret the conditions as if they were intended to trick you. For example, if a question asks how many people could be eligible to serve on a committee, consider only those people named in the passage unless directed otherwise. When in doubt, read the conditions in their most obvious sense. Remember, however, that the language in the conditions is intended to be read for precise meaning. It is essential to pay particular attention to words that describe or limit relationships, such as "only," "exactly," "never," "always," "must be," "cannot be," and the like.

The result of this careful reading will be a clear picture of the structure of the relationships involved, including the kinds of relationships permitted, the participants in the relationships, and the range of possible actions or attributes for these participants.

Keep in mind question independence. Each question should be considered separately from the other questions in its set. No information, except what is given in the original conditions, should be carried over from one question to another.

In some cases a question will simply ask for conclusions to be drawn from the conditions as originally given. Some questions may, however, add information to the original conditions or temporarily suspend or replace one of the original conditions for the purpose of that question only. For example, if Question 1 adds the supposition "if P is sitting at table 2 ...," this supposition should NOT be carried over to any other question in the set.

Consider highlighting text and using diagrams. Many people find it useful to underline key points in the passage and in each question. In addition, it may prove very helpful to draw a diagram to assist you in finding the solution to the problem.

In preparing for the test, you may wish to experiment with different types of diagrams. For a scheduling problem, a simple calendar-like diagram may be helpful. For a grouping problem, an array of labeled columns or rows may be useful.

Even though most people find diagrams to be very helpful, some people seldom use them, and for some individual questions no one will need a diagram. There is by no means universal agreement on which kind of diagram is best for which problem or in which cases a diagram is most useful. Do not be concerned if a particular problem in the test seems to be best approached without the use of a diagram.

Logical Reasoning Questions

Arguments are a fundamental part of the law, and analyzing arguments is a key element of legal analysis. Training in the law builds on a foundation of basic reasoning skills. Law students must draw on the skills of analyzing, evaluating, constructing, and refuting arguments. They need to be able to identify what information is relevant to an issue or argument and what impact further evidence might have. They need to be able to reconcile opposing positions and use arguments to persuade others.

Logical Reasoning questions evaluate the ability to analyze, critically evaluate, and complete arguments as they occur in ordinary language. The questions are based on short arguments drawn from a wide variety of sources, including newspapers, general interest magazines, scholarly publications, advertisements, and informal discourse. These arguments mirror legal reasoning in the types of arguments presented and in their complexity, though few of the arguments actually have law as a subject matter.

Each Logical Reasoning question requires you to read and comprehend a short passage, then answer one question (or, rarely, two questions) about it. The questions are designed to assess a wide range of skills involved in thinking critically, with an emphasis on skills that are central to legal reasoning.

These skills include:

- Recognizing the parts of an argument and their relationships

- Recognizing similarities and differences between patterns of reasoning

- Drawing well-supported conclusions

- Reasoning by analogy

- Recognizing misunderstandings or points of disagreement

- Determining how additional evidence affects an argument

- Detecting assumptions made by particular arguments

- Identifying and applying principles or rules

- Identifying flaws in arguments

- Identifying explanations

The questions do not presuppose specialized knowledge of logical terminology. For example, you will not be expected to know the meaning of specialized terms such as "ad hominem" or "syllogism." On the other hand, you will be expected to understand and critique the reasoning contained in arguments. This requires that you possess a university-level understanding of widely used concepts such as argument, premise, assumption, and conclusion.

Suggested Approach
Read each question carefully. Make sure that you understand the meaning of each part of the question. Make sure that you understand the meaning of each answer choice and the ways in which it may or may not relate to the question posed.

Do not pick a response simply because it is a true statement. Although true, it may not answer the question posed.

Answer each question on the basis of the information that is given, even if you do not agree with it. Work within the context provided by the passage. LSAT questions do not involve any tricks or hidden meanings.

Reading Comprehension Questions

Both law school and the practice of law revolve around extensive reading of highly varied, dense, argumentative, and expository texts (for example, cases, codes, contracts, briefs, decisions, evidence). This reading must be exacting, distinguishing precisely what is said from what is not said. It involves comparison, analysis, synthesis, and application (for example, of principles and rules). It involves drawing appropriate inferences and applying ideas and arguments to new contexts. Law school reading also requires the ability to grasp unfamiliar subject matter and the ability to penetrate difficult and challenging material.

The purpose of LSAT Reading Comprehension questions is to measure the ability to read, with understanding and insight, examples of lengthy and complex materials similar to those commonly encountered in law school. The Reading Comprehension section of the LSAT contains four sets of reading questions, each set consisting of a selection of reading material followed by five to eight questions. The reading selection in three of the four sets consists of a single reading passage; the other set contains two related shorter passages. Sets with two passages are a variant of Reading Comprehension called Comparative Reading, which was introduced in June 2007.

Comparative Reading questions concern the relationships between the two passages, such as those of generalization/instance, principle/application, or point/counterpoint. Law school work often requires reading two or more texts in conjunction with each other and understanding their relationships. For example, a law student may read a trial court decision together with an appellate court decision that overturns it, or identify the fact pattern from a hypothetical suit together with the potentially controlling case law.

Reading selections for LSAT Reading Comprehension questions are drawn from a wide range of subjects in the humanities, the social sciences, the biological and physical sciences, and areas related to the law. Generally, the selections are densely written, use high-level vocabulary, and contain sophisticated argument or complex rhetorical structure (for example, multiple points of view). Reading Comprehension questions require you to read carefully and accurately, to determine the relationships among the various parts of the reading selection, and to draw reasonable inferences from the material in the selection. The questions may ask about the following characteristics of a passage or pair of passages:

- The main idea or primary purpose

- Information that is explicitly stated

- Information or ideas that can be inferred

- The meaning or purpose of words or phrases as used in context

- The organization or structure

- The application of information in the selection to a new context

- Principles that function in the selection

- Analogies to claims or arguments in the selection

- An author's attitude as revealed in the tone of a passage or the language used

- The impact of new information on claims or arguments in the selection

Suggested Approach

Since reading selections are drawn from many different disciplines and sources, you should not be discouraged if you encounter material with which you are not familiar. It is important to remember that questions are to be answered exclusively on the basis of the information provided in the selection. There is no particular knowledge that you are expected to bring to the test, and you should not make inferences based on any prior knowledge of a subject that you may have. You may, however, wish to defer working on a set of questions that seems particularly difficult or unfamiliar until after you have dealt with sets you find easier.

Strategies. One question that often arises in connection with Reading Comprehension has to do with the most effective and efficient order in which to read the selections and questions. Possible approaches include:

- reading the selection very closely and then answering the questions;

- reading the questions first, reading the selection closely, and then returning to the questions; or

- skimming the selection and questions very quickly, then rereading the selection closely and answering the questions.

Test takers are different, and the best strategy for one might not be the best strategy for another. In preparing for the test, therefore, you might want to experiment with the different strategies and decide what works most effectively for you.

Remember that your strategy must be effective under timed conditions. For this reason, the first strategy— reading the selection very closely and then answering the questions—may be the most effective for you. Nonetheless, if you believe that one of the other strategies

might be more effective for you, you should try it out and assess your performance using it.

Reading the selection. Whatever strategy you choose, you should give the passage or pair of passages at least one careful reading before answering the questions. Try to distinguish main ideas from supporting ideas, and opinions or attitudes from factual, objective information. Note transitions from one idea to the next and identify the relationships among the different ideas or parts of a passage, or between the two passages in Comparative Reading sets. Consider how and why an author makes points and draws conclusions. Be sensitive to implications of what the passages say.

You may find it helpful to mark key parts of passages. For example, you might underline main ideas or important arguments, and you might circle transitional words— "although," "nevertheless," "correspondingly," and the like—that will help you map the structure of a passage. Also, you might note descriptive words that will help you identify an author's attitude toward a particular idea or person.

Answering the Questions

- Always read all the answer choices before selecting the best answer. The best answer choice is the one that most accurately and completely answers the question being posed.

- Respond to the specific question being asked. Do not pick an answer choice simply because it is a true statement. For example, picking a true statement might yield an incorrect answer to a question in which you are asked to identify an author's position on an issue, since you are not being asked to evaluate the truth of the author's position but only to correctly identify what that position is.

- Answer the questions only on the basis of the information provided in the selection. Your own views, interpretations, or opinions, and those you have heard from others, may sometimes conflict with those expressed in a reading selection; however, you are expected to work within the context provided by the reading selection. You should not expect to agree with everything you encounter in Reading Comprehension passages.

THE WRITING SAMPLE

On the day of the test, you will be asked to write one sample essay. LSAC does not score the writing sample, but copies are sent to all law schools to which you apply. According to a 2006 LSAC survey of 157 United States and Canadian law schools, almost all use the writing sample in evaluating at least some applications for admission. Failure to respond to writing sample prompts and frivolous responses have been used by law schools as grounds for rejection of applications for admission.

In developing and implementing the writing sample portion of the LSAT, LSAC has operated on the following premises: First, law schools and the legal profession value highly the ability to communicate effectively in writing. Second, it is important to encourage potential law students to develop effective writing skills. Third, a sample of an applicant's writing, produced under controlled conditions, is a potentially useful indication of that person's writing ability. Fourth, the writing sample can serve as an independent check on other writing submitted by applicants as part of the admission process. Finally, writing samples may be useful for diagnostic purposes related to improving a candidate's writing.

The writing prompt presents a decision problem. You are asked to make a choice between two positions or courses of action. Both of the choices are defensible, and you are given criteria and facts on which to base your decision. There is no "right" or "wrong" position to take on the topic, so the quality of each test taker's response is a function not of which choice is made, but of how well or poorly the choice is supported and how well or poorly the other choice is criticized.

The LSAT writing prompt was designed and validated by legal education professionals. Since it involves writing based on fact sets and criteria, the writing sample gives applicants the opportunity to demonstrate the type of argumentative writing that is required in law school, although the topics are usually nonlegal.

You will have 35 minutes in which to plan and write an essay on the topic you receive. Read the topic and the accompanying directions carefully. You will probably find it best to spend a few minutes considering the topic and organizing your thoughts before you begin writing. In your essay, be sure to develop your ideas fully, leaving time, if possible, to review what you have written. Do not write on a topic other than the one specified. Writing on a topic of your own choice is not acceptable.

No special knowledge is required or expected for this writing exercise. Law schools are interested in the reasoning, clarity, organization, language usage, and writing mechanics displayed in your essay. How well you write is more important than how much you write. Confine your essay to the blocked, lined area on the front and back of the separate Writing Sample Response Sheet. Only that area will be reproduced for law schools. Be sure that your writing is legible.

TAKING THE PREPTEST UNDER SIMULATED LSAT CONDITIONS

One important way to prepare for the LSAT is to simulate the day of the test by taking a practice test under actual time constraints. Taking a practice test under timed conditions helps you to estimate the amount of time you can afford to spend on each question in a section and to determine the question types on which you may need additional practice.

Since the LSAT is a timed test, it is important to use your allotted time wisely. During the test, you may work only on the section designated by the test supervisor. You cannot devote extra time to a difficult section and make up that time on a section you find easier. In pacing yourself, and checking your answers, you should think of each section of the test as a separate minitest.

Be sure that you answer every question on the test. When you do not know the correct answer to a question, first eliminate the responses that you know are incorrect, then make your best guess among the remaining choices. Do not be afraid to guess as there is no penalty for incorrect answers.

When you take a practice test, abide by all the requirements specified in the directions and keep strictly within the specified time limits. Work without a rest period. When you take an actual test, you will have only a short break—usually 10-15 minutes—after SECTION III.

When taken under conditions as much like actual testing conditions as possible, a practice test provides very useful preparation for taking the LSAT.

Official directions for the four multiple-choice sections and the writing sample are included in this PrepTest so that you can approximate actual testing conditions as you practice.

To take the test:

- Set a timer for 35 minutes. Answer all the questions in SECTION I of this PrepTest. Stop working on that section when the 35 minutes have elapsed.

- Repeat, allowing yourself 35 minutes each for sections II, III, and IV.

- Set the timer again for 35 minutes, then prepare your response to the writing sample topic at the end of this PrepTest.

- Refer to "Computing Your Score" for the PrepTest for instruction on evaluating your performance. An answer key is provided for that purpose.

The practice test that follows consists of four sections corresponding to the four scored sections of the June 2012 LSAT. Also reprinted is the June 2012 unscored writing sample topic.

General Directions for the LSAT Answer Sheet

The actual testing time for this portion of the test will be 2 hours 55 minutes. There are five sections, each with a time limit of 35 minutes. The supervisor will tell you when to begin and end each section. If you finish a section before time is called, you may check your work on that section only; do not turn to any other section of the test book and do not work on any other section either in the test book or on the answer sheet.

There are several different types of questions on the test, and each question type has its own directions. Be sure you understand the directions for each question type before attempting to answer any questions in that section.

Not everyone will finish all the questions in the time allowed. Do not hurry, but work steadily and as quickly as you can without sacrificing accuracy. You are advised to use your time effectively. If a question seems too difficult, go on to the next one and return to the difficult question after completing the section. MARK THE BEST ANSWER YOU CAN FOR EVERY QUESTION. NO DEDUCTIONS WILL BE MADE FOR WRONG ANSWERS. YOUR SCORE WILL BE BASED ONLY ON THE NUMBER OF QUESTIONS YOU ANSWER CORRECTLY.

ALL YOUR ANSWERS MUST BE MARKED ON THE ANSWER SHEET. Answer spaces for each question are lettered to correspond with the letters of the potential answers to each question in the test book. After you have decided which of the answers is correct, blacken the corresponding space on the answer sheet. BE SURE THAT EACH MARK IS BLACK AND COMPLETELY FILLS THE ANSWER SPACE. Give only one answer to each question. If you change an answer, be sure that all previous marks are erased completely. Since the answer sheet is machine scored, incomplete erasures may be interpreted as intended answers. ANSWERS RECORDED IN THE TEST BOOK WILL NOT BE SCORED.

There may be more question numbers on this answer sheet than there are questions in a section. Do not be concerned, but be certain that the section and number of the question you are answering matches the answer sheet section and question number. Additional answer spaces in any answer sheet section should be left blank. Begin your next section in the number one answer space for that section.

LSAC takes various steps to ensure that answer sheets are returned from test centers in a timely manner for processing. In the unlikely event that an answer sheet is not received, LSAC will permit the examinee either to retest at no additional fee or to receive a refund of his or her LSAT fee. THESE REMEDIES ARE THE ONLY REMEDIES AVAILABLE IN THE UNLIKELY EVENT THAT AN ANSWER SHEET IS NOT RECEIVED BY LSAC.

Score Cancellation

Complete this section only if you are absolutely certain you want to cancel your score. A CANCELLATION REQUEST CANNOT BE RESCINDED. IF YOU ARE AT ALL UNCERTAIN, YOU SHOULD NOT COMPLETE THIS SECTION.

To cancel your score from this administration, you **must:**

A. fill in both ovals here ..... ○ ○
        AND

B. read the following statement. Then sign your name and enter the date.
    YOUR SIGNATURE ALONE IS NOT SUFFICIENT FOR SCORE CANCELLATION. BOTH OVALS ABOVE MUST BE FILLED IN FOR SCANNING EQUIPMENT TO RECOGNIZE YOUR REQUEST FOR SCORE CANCELLATION.

I certify that I wish to cancel my test score from this administration. I understand that my request is irreversible and that my score will not be sent to me or to the law schools to which I apply.

_____
Sign your name in full

_____
Date

FOR LSAC USE ONLY   ●

HOW DID YOU PREPARE FOR THE LSAT?
(Select all that apply.)

Responses to this item are voluntary and will be used for statistical research purposes only.

○ By studying the free sample questions available on LSAC's website.
○ By taking the free sample LSAT available on LSAC's website.
○ By working through official LSAT *PrepTests, ItemWise,* and/or other LSAC test prep products.
○ By using LSAT prep books or software **not** published by LSAC.
○ By attending a commercial test preparation or coaching course.
○ By attending a test preparation or coaching course offered through an undergraduate institution.
○ Self study.
○ Other preparation.
○ No preparation.

CERTIFYING STATEMENT

Please write the following statement. Sign and date.

I certify that I am the examinee whose name appears on this answer sheet and that I am here to take the LSAT for the sole purpose of being considered for admission to law school. I further certify that I will neither assist nor receive assistance from any other candidate, and I agree not to copy, retain, or transmit examination questions in any form or discuss them with any other person.

_____
_____
_____
_____
_____
_____
_____
_____
_____

SIGNATURE: _____   TODAY'S DATE: ___/___/___
                                                                                    MONTH DAY YEAR

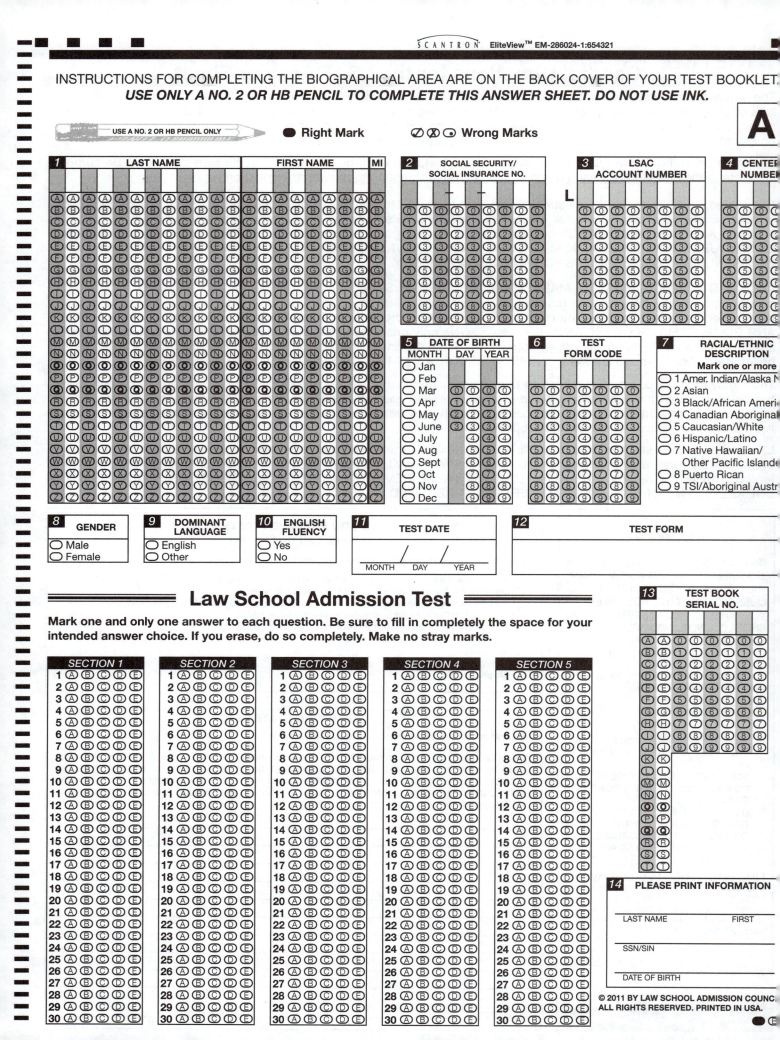

THE PREPTEST

SECTION I

Time—35 minutes

27 Questions

Directions: Each set of questions in this section is based on a single passage or a pair of passages. The questions are to be answered on the basis of what is stated or implied in the passage or pair of passages. For some of the questions, more than one of the choices could conceivably answer the question. However, you are to choose the best answer; that is, the response that most accurately and completely answers the question, and blacken the corresponding space on your answer sheet.

The Internet makes possible the instantaneous transmission and retrieval of digital text. It is widely assumed that this capacity will lead to the displacement of printed books by digitized books that are read
(5) mainly on computer screens or handheld electronic devices. But it is more likely, I believe, that most digital files of books will be printed and bound on demand at point of sale by machines that can quickly and inexpensively make single copies that are
(10) indistinguishable from books made in factories. Once most books have been digitized, anyone with access to the Internet will be able to purchase printed books from a practically limitless digital catalog that includes even those books that, under traditional publishing
(15) assumptions, would have been designated "out of print."

Also, the digital publication of a book online involves no physical inventory, thereby eliminating the costs of warehousing, shipping books to wholesalers and to retail stores, displaying physical books in retail
(20) stores, and returning unsold books to publishers. This would make digital publishing much less expensive than traditional publishing. Given the economic efficiency and convenience for customers of this new digital model of publishing, it is likely to eventually
(25) supplant or at least rival traditional publishing— although it will be some time before a catalog of printable digitized books becomes large enough to justify investment in book printing machines at numerous regional sites.
(30) Moreover, the elimination of whole categories of expense means that under the digital publishing model, authors would be responsible for a greater proportion of the value of the final product and would therefore, according to literary agents, be entitled to a larger
(35) share of the proceeds. Currently a large percentage of publishers' revenue is absorbed by the costs of printing, selling, and distributing physical books, costs that are irrelevant to digital publication. Literary agents marketing new manuscripts could thus be expected
(40) to demand a significantly bigger slice of revenue for their authors than has been traditional. But large, established publishing houses, which are heavily invested in the infrastructure of traditional publishing, initially will be reluctant to accede. So the opportunity
(45) to bid for new manuscripts will go first to upstart digital-publishing firms unfettered by traditional practices or infrastructure. Under this competitive pressure, traditional publishers will have to reduce their redundant functions in order to accommodate
(50) higher royalty payments to authors or else they will

lose their authors. Such adjustments are typical of the interval between a departing economic model and its successor and may help explain the caution with which today's publishing conglomerates are approaching
(55) the digital future.

1. Which one of the following statements most accurately expresses the main point of the passage?

(A) The shift from traditional to digital publishing is typical of the shift from one economic model to a more efficient economic model.

(B) Digital publishing is likely to one day rival traditional publishing, but social and economic factors are currently hindering its acceptance.

(C) Digital publishing will be convenient for readers and profitable for publishers but will also result in a great deal of movement by authors among different publishing houses.

(D) Although digital books can now be displayed on computers and handheld electronic devices, consumers will demonstrate that they prefer books printed at the point of sale.

(E) Digital publishing will transform the economics of the publishing business and in doing so will likely create competitive pressures to pay authors a greater percentage of publishers' net revenue.

2. The author uses the phrase "whole categories of expense" (lines 30–31) primarily to refer to

(A) the fees collected by literary agents from their clients

(B) the price paid to have books printed and bound

(C) the royalties paid to authors by their publishers

(D) the costs specific to the retail trade in traditional printed books

(E) the total sales of a book minus the value of those books returned unsold to the bookseller

GO ON TO THE NEXT PAGE.

3. It can most reasonably be inferred that the author would agree with which one of the following statements?

(A) Those publishers that fail to embrace the new digital model of publishing will be unlikely to remain economically competitive.
(B) The primary threat to the spread of digital publishing will be the widespread use of computers and handheld devices for reading text.
(C) The growth of digital publishing is likely to revitalize the book retail business.
(D) Any book will sell more copies if it is published digitally than if it is published traditionally.
(E) Digital publishing will allow publishers to substantially decrease the amount of money they allocate for advertising their books.

4. Each of the following is identified in the passage as something digital publishing will dispense with the need for EXCEPT:

(A) warehousing printed books
(B) having book covers designed
(C) having books shipped to retail stores
(D) having unsold books returned to publishers
(E) displaying books in retail stores

5. If the scenario described in the first two paragraphs were to become true, then which one of the following would most likely be the case?

(A) The need for warehousing will shift mainly from that of individual books to that of paper and binding material to make books.
(B) The patronage of stores that sell used books will increase significantly.
(C) Most publishers will sell their own books individually and will not use distributors or retailers.
(D) There will be significantly less demand by publishers for the services of copy editors and book designers.
(E) The demand for book-grade paper will decrease significantly.

6. It can most reasonably be inferred that the author would agree with which one of the following statements?

(A) The changing literary tastes of consumers will be the main cause of the eventual transition to the new digital model.
(B) The ease of keeping books "in print" will be the primary factor in the eventual acceptance of the new digital model.
(C) The demands of literary agents will be the impetus for completing the transition to the new digital model.
(D) The development of innovative marketing strategies will ensure acceptance of the new digital model.
(E) Widespread familiarity with new ways of storing information will be the primary reason for the acceptance of the new digital model.

7. The primary purpose of the final sentence of the passage is to

(A) suggest that traditional publishing houses have been too slow to embrace digital publishing
(B) provide a broader context that helps to clarify the situation facing traditional publishers
(C) summarize the argument for the claim that digital publishing will likely replace traditional publishing
(D) illustrate the primary obstacle facing traditional publishing houses that wish to incorporate digital publishing capabilities
(E) recommend a wait-and-see approach on the part of traditional publishing houses

GO ON TO THE NEXT PAGE.

Passage A

In this appeal of his criminal conviction, the defendant challenges the fingerprint evidence used against him at trial, claiming that fingerprint identification theory has not been adequately tested.
(5) He cites the inability of the fingerprint examiner who incriminated him at trial to name any studies establishing that no two persons have identical fingerprints.

The defendant claims that there are no established error rates revealing how often fingerprint examiners
(10) incorrectly identify a fingerprint as a particular person's, and asserts that fingerprint examiners lack uniform, objective standards. He cites testimony given by the fingerprint examiner at trial that there is no generally accepted standard regarding the number of "points of
(15) identification" required for a positive identification.

Although fingerprint identification has not attained the status of scientific law, it has been used in criminal trials for 100 years, and experts have long concurred about its reliability. While further testing
(20) and the development of even more consistent standards may be desirable, this court sees no reason to reject outright a form of evidence that has so ably withstood the test of time.

While it may be true that different agencies
(25) require different degrees of correlation before permitting a positive identification, fingerprint examiners are held to a consistent "points and characteristics" approach to identification. As the fingerprint expert testified at the defendant's trial,
(30) examiners are regularly subjected to testing and proficiency requirements, and uniform standards have been established through professional training and peer review. The trial court below was therefore within its discretion in crediting testimony that fingerprint
(35) identification has an exceedingly low error rate.

Passage B

Fingerprint examiners lack objective standards for evaluating whether two prints "match." There is simply no consensus about what constitutes a sufficient basis for identification. Some examiners use a "point-
(40) counting" method that entails counting the number of similar "ridge" characteristics on prints, but there is no fixed requirement about how many points of similarity are needed, and local practices vary. Others reject point counting for a more holistic approach. Either
(45) way, there is no generally agreed-on standard for determining precisely when to declare a match.

Although we know that different individuals can share certain ridge characteristics, the chance of two individuals sharing any given number of identifying
(50) characteristics is unknown. How likely is it that two people could have four points of resemblance, or five, or eight? Moreover, fingerprints used in forensic identification are typically partial and smudged. Are the odds that two partial prints from different people
(55) will match one in a thousand, one in a million, or one in a billion? No fingerprint examiner can answer such questions decisively, yet the answers are critical to evaluating the value of fingerprint evidence.

The error rate for fingerprint identification in
(60) actual practice has received little systematic study. How often do fingerprint examiners mistakenly declare a match? Although some proficiency tests show examiners making few or no errors, these tests have been criticized as lax; a more rigorous test
(65) showed a 34 percent rate of erroneous identification.

8. Which one of the following most accurately expresses the main point of passage B?

    (A) Criminal defendants do not always have a full and fair opportunity to challenge faulty fingerprint evidence when it is used against them at trial.
    (B) Fingerprint evidence has been shown to be too unreliable for use in criminal trials.
    (C) The error rate for fingerprint identification is significantly higher than is generally acknowledged.
    (D) There are a number of fundamental problems in the field of fingerprint identification as it is currently practiced.
    (E) There is a growing consensus within the legal community that fingerprint evidence is often unreliable.

9. The authors would be most likely to disagree about

    (A) whether uniformity in the training of fingerprint examiners is desirable
    (B) the likelihood that a fingerprint examiner will incorrectly declare a match in a given criminal case
    (C) whether fingerprint identification should be accorded the status of scientific law
    (D) the relative merits of the point-counting and holistic methods of fingerprint identification
    (E) whether different agencies vary in the degree of correlation they require for examiners to declare a match

10. It can be inferred that the author of passage A is

    (A) a judge presiding over an appeal of a criminal conviction
    (B) a defense attorney arguing an appeal of a client's criminal conviction
    (C) a prosecutor arguing for the affirmation of a guilty verdict
    (D) a professor of law lecturing to a criminal law class
    (E) an academic presenting a paper to a group of legal scholars

GO ON TO THE NEXT PAGE.

11. Each passage discusses the relationship between the reliability of the practice of fingerprint identification and which one of the following?

(A) the ability of a criminal defendant to expose weaknesses in the prosecution's case

(B) the personal integrity of individual fingerprint examiners

(C) differences in the identification practices used by various fingerprint examiners

(D) the partial or smudged prints that are typically used as evidence in criminal cases

(E) use of the holistic approach to fingerprint identification

12. Which one of the following principles underlies the arguments in both passages?

(A) Courts should be extremely reluctant to reject those forms of evidence that have withstood the test of time.

(B) Defendants should have the right to challenge forms of evidence whose reliability has not been scientifically proven.

(C) To evaluate the value of fingerprint evidence, one must know how likely it is that partial prints from two different people would match.

(D) Fingerprint identification should not be considered to have a low error rate unless rigorously conducted tests have shown this to be so.

(E) Fingerprint examiners must follow objective standards if fingerprint identification is to be reliable.

13. Both passages allude to a method of fingerprint identification in which examiners

(A) rely on a holistic impression of how similar two fingerprints are

(B) use computerized databases to search for matching fingerprints

(C) count the number of characteristics two fingerprints have in common

(D) calculate the odds of two different individuals' sharing certain very rare fingerprint characteristics

(E) use computer technology to clarify the images of smudged or partial fingerprints

14. Passage B differs from passage A in that passage B is more

(A) optimistic in its conclusions
(B) general in focus
(C) tentative in its claims
(D) respectful of opposing claims
(E) dependent on unsubstantiated assumptions

GO ON TO THE NEXT PAGE.

Music and literature, rivals among the arts, have not coexisted without intruding on each other's terrain. Ever since what we think of as "literature" developed out of the sounds of spoken, sung, and chanted art,
(5) writing has aspired to the condition of music, in which form contributes significantly to content. Nowhere is this truer than in the African American tradition, whose music is often considered its greatest artistic achievement and one of the greatest contributions to
(10) North American art. But while many African American writers have used musicians and music as theme and metaphor in their writing, none had attempted to draw upon a musical genre as the structuring principle for an entire novel until Toni Morrison did so in her 1992
(15) novel *Jazz*, a novel set in the Harlem section of New York City in 1926.

In *Jazz*, the connection to music is found not only in the novel's plot but, more strikingly, in the way in which the story is told. The narration slips easily from
(20) the third-person omniscience of the narrator's disembodied voice—which, though sensitive and sympathetic, claims no particular identity, gender, or immersion in specific social circumstances—to the first-person lyricism of key characters. But throughout
(25) these shifts, the narrator is both generous with the characters' voices and protective of his or her mastery over the narrative as a whole. On the one hand, the central characters are given the responsibility of relating their parts of the overarching story, but on
(30) the other hand, their sections are set off by quotation marks, reminders that the narrator is allowing them to speak. In this way, the narrative is analogous in structure to the playing of a jazz band which intertwines its ensemble sound with the individuality
(35) of embedded solo performances.

In jazz, composer and conductor Duke Ellington was the first to construct his compositions with his individual musicians and their unique "voices" in mind. Yet no matter how lengthy his musicians'
(40) improvisations, no matter how bold or inventive their solos might be, they always performed within the undeniable logic of the composer's frame—they always, in other words, performed as if with quotation marks around their improvisations and solos. It is this
(45) same effect that Toni Morrison has achieved in *Jazz*, a literary rendering of an art of composition that Duke Ellington perfected around the time in which *Jazz* is set.

In this novel, Morrison has found a way,
(50) paradoxically, to create the sense of an ensemble of characters improvising within the fixed scope of a carefully constructed collective narration. By simulating the style of a genius of music while exhibiting Morrison's own linguistic virtuosity,
(55) *Jazz* serves to redefine the very possibilities of narrative point of view.

15. Which one of the following most accurately states the main point of the passage?

(A) In *Jazz*, Morrison has realized a significant artistic achievement in creating the first African American work of fiction whose plot, themes, and setting are all drawn from the world of jazz.

(B) Morrison's striking description of a musical ensemble performance containing solo improvisations constitutes an important artistic innovation and makes *Jazz* an important model for other writers.

(C) Although many African American writers have used music as a central metaphor in their works, Morrison's 1992 novel is unique and innovative for using jazz as its central metaphor.

(D) Building on the works of many African American writers and musical composers, Morrison has over the years developed an innovative jazzlike style of narration, which she used especially effectively in the novel *Jazz*.

(E) In *Jazz*, Morrison has succeeded in creating an original and effective narrative strategy that is a literary analogue of Duke Ellington's style of musical composition.

16. The author's discussion in the first paragraph proceeds in which one of the following ways?

(A) from a common claim about the arts, to a denial of this claim as applied to a particular artistic tradition, to a hypothesis about a particular individual

(B) from a general remark about two art forms, to a similar observation about a particular artistic tradition, to a specific comment about a particular work that exemplifies the prior remarks

(C) from a description of a common claim about two art forms, to some specific evidence that supports that claim, to an inference regarding a particular individual to whom that claim applies

(D) from an observation about a specific art form, to a more general claim about the applicability of that observation to other art forms, to a particular counterexample to the first observation

(E) from general comments about the arts, to a purported counterexample to the general comments as applied to a particular artistic tradition, to a description of a particular work that bears out the original comments

GO ON TO THE NEXT PAGE.

17. The author's assertion in lines 10–16 would be most called into question if which one of the following were true?

(A)   Even a casual reading of *Jazz* makes it evident that the author has intentionally tried to simulate a style of jazz performance in the narration of the story.

(B)   A small number of African American novelists writing earlier in the twentieth century sought to base the form of their work on the typical structure of blues music.

(C)   All novels about nonliterary arts and artists appear as if their authors have tried to make their narrative styles reminiscent of the arts in question.

(D)   Depending partly on whether or not it is read aloud, any novel can be found to be somewhat musical in nature.

(E)   A smaller number of African American writers than of non-African American writers in North America have written novels whose plots and characters have to do with music.

18. The information in the passage most supports which one of the following statements regarding Ellington?

(A)   Morrison has explicitly credited him with inspiring the style of narration that she developed in *Jazz*.

(B)   He prevented his musicians from performing lengthy solos in order to preserve the unity of his compositions.

(C)   He is a minor character in Morrison's *Jazz*.

(D)   He composed music that was originally intended to be performed by the specific musicians he conducted.

(E)   Though he composed and conducted primarily jazz, he also composed some music of other genres.

19. The author's primary purpose in the passage is to

(A)   analyze and commend the variety of contributions to the art of the novel made by a particular writer

(B)   contrast a particular African American writer's work with the work of African American practitioners of another art

(C)   describe a particular aspect of one work by a particular writer

(D)   demonstrate the ways in which two apparently dissimilar arts are, on a deeper analysis, actually quite similar

(E)   detail the thematic concerns in the work of a particular writer and identify the sources of those concerns

20. Each of the following excerpts from the passage exhibits the author's attitude toward the novel *Jazz* EXCEPT:

(A)   "...whose music is often considered its greatest artistic achievement and one of the greatest contributions to North American art" (lines 8–10)

(B)   "In *Jazz*, the connection to music is found not only in the novel's plot but, more strikingly, in the way in which the story is told" (lines 17–19)

(C)   "The narration slips easily from the third-person omniscience of the narrator's disembodied voice..." (lines 19–21)

(D)   "...Morrison has found a way, paradoxically, to create the sense of an ensemble of characters improvising within the fixed scope..." (lines 49–51)

(E)   "By simulating the style of a genius of music while exhibiting Morrison's own linguistic virtuosity..." (lines 52–54)

21. It can be inferred from the passage that the author would be most likely to believe which one of the following?

(A)   In *Jazz*, Morrison has perfected a style of narration that had been attempted with little success by other North American writers in the twentieth century.

(B)   Because of its use of narrative techniques inspired by jazz, Morrison's novel represents the most successful representation to date of the milieu in which jazz musicians live and work.

(C)   In *Jazz*, Morrison develops her narrative in such a way that the voices of individual characters are sometimes difficult to distinguish, in much the same way that individual musicians' voices merge in ensemble jazz playing.

(D)   The structural analogy between *Jazz* and Duke Ellington's compositional style involves more than simply the technique of shifting between first-person and third-person narrators.

(E)   Morrison disguises the important structural connections between her narrative and Duke Ellington's jazz compositions by making the transitions between first- and third-person narrators appear easy.

22. The passage contains information that most helps to answer which one of the following questions?

(A)   Do any African American visual artists also attempt to emulate African American music in their work?

(B)   In what way is *Jazz* stylistically similar to other literary works by Morrison?

(C)   After the publication of *Jazz*, did critics quickly acknowledge the innovative nature of the narrative style that Morrison uses in that novel?

(D)   How many works by African American writers have been inspired by the music of Duke Ellington?

(E)   What characteristic of *Jazz* is also present in the work of some other African American writers?

GO ON TO THE NEXT PAGE.

Advances in scientific understanding often do not build directly or smoothly in response to the data that are amassed, and in retrospect, after a major revision of theory, it may seem strange that a crucial hypothesis

(5) was long overlooked. A case in point is the discovery of a means by which the nuclei of atoms can be split. Between 1934, when a group of Italian physicists including Enrico Fermi first bombarded uranium with neutrons, and 1939, when exiled Austrian physicist

(10) Lise Meitner provided the crucial theoretical connection, scientists compiled increasing evidence that nuclear fission had been achieved, without, however, recognizing what they were witnessing.

Earlier, even before the neutron and proton

(15) composition of atomic nuclei had been experimentally demonstrated, some theoretical physicists had produced calculations indicating that in principle it should be possible to break atoms apart. But the neutron-bombardment experiments were not aimed at

(20) achieving such a result, and researchers were not even receptive to the possibility that it might happen in that context. A common view was that a neutron's breaking apart a uranium nucleus would be analogous to a pebble, thrown through a window, causing a house

(25) to collapse.

In Berlin, Meitner pursued research related to that of the Italians, discovering a puzzling group of radioactive substances produced by neutron bombardment of uranium. Fermi and others achieved

(30) numerous similar results. These products remained unidentified partly because precise chemical analyses were hampered by the minute quantities of the substances produced and the dangers of working with highly radioactive materials, but more significantly

(35) because of the expectation that they would all be elements close to uranium in nuclear composition. In 1938 Meitner escaped from Nazi Germany and undertook related research in Sweden, but her research partner Otto Hahn kept her informed of his continuing

(40) experimentation. Late in that year he wrote to her of a surprising result: one of the substances resulting from the neutron bombardment of uranium had been conclusively identified as barium, an element whose structure would have made it impossible to produce

(45) through any mechanism he envisaged as being involved in the experiments. Hahn even remarked that, despite the clear chemical evidence of what had occurred, it went "against all previous experiences of nuclear physics," but he also noted that together the

(50) number of protons and neutrons in the nuclei of barium and technetium, the accompanying product of the experiment, added up to the number of such particles that compose a uranium nucleus.

It was Meitner who finally recognized the

(55) significance of the data in relation to underlying theoretical considerations: the researchers had actually been splitting uranium atoms. Coining the term "nuclear fission," she quickly submitted her conclusion for publication in a paper coauthored with

(60) physicist Otto Frisch. When scientists in Europe and North America rushed to corroborate the findings, it became clear that the relevant evidence had been present for some time, lacking mainly the right conceptual link.

23. The author's primary aim in the passage is to

(A) criticize a traditional view of scientific progress and advocate a replacement
(B) illustrate the often erratic way in which a scientific community achieves progress
(C) judge the relative importance of theory and experimentation in science
(D) take issue with the idea that scientists make slow, steady progress
(E) display the way in which intellectual arrogance sometimes hinders scientific progress

24. The most likely reason that the theoretical physicists in line 16 would have been pleased about Meitner's insight regarding the neutron bombardment experiments is that her insight

(A) was dependent upon the calculations that they had produced
(B) paved the way for work in theoretical physics to become more acceptable abroad
(C) proved that the nuclei of atoms were generally unstable
(D) confirmed their earlier work indicating that atoms could be split
(E) came after years of analyzing the data from experiments conducted between 1934 and 1938

25. Which one of the following is most nearly equivalent to what the author means by "the relevant evidence" (line 62)?

(A) the results of experiments in neutron bombardment of uranium conducted by the physics community between 1934 and 1939
(B) the results of related experiments in neutron bombardment of uranium conducted by Meitner in 1938
(C) the clear chemical evidence that Hahn had found of barium's being produced by neutron bombardment of uranium
(D) the fact that the sum of the number of protons and neutrons in the nuclei of barium and technetium was the same as the number of these particles in a uranium nucleus
(E) the fact that radioactive products of neutron bombardment of uranium went unidentified for so long

GO ON TO THE NEXT PAGE.

26. Given the information in the passage, which one of the following, if true, would have been most likely to reduce the amount of time it took for physicists to realize that atoms were being split?

(A) The physicists conducting the experiments in neutron bombardment of uranium were all using the same research techniques.

(B) The physicists conducting the experiments in neutron bombardment of uranium did not have particular expectations regarding the likely nuclear composition of the by-products.

(C) The physicists conducting the experiments in neutron bombardment of uranium had not been aware of the calculations indicating that in principle it was possible to split atoms.

(D) More physicists concentrated on obtaining experimental results from the neutron bombardment of uranium.

(E) Physicists conducted experiments in the neutron bombardment of some substance other than uranium.

27. According to the passage, which one of the following was true of the physics community during the 1930s?

(A) It neglected earlier theoretical developments.

(B) It reevaluated calculations indicating that atoms could be split.

(C) It never identified the by-products of neutron bombardment of uranium.

(D) It showed that uranium atoms were the easiest to split.

(E) It recognized the dangers of working with radioactive substances.

S T O P

IF YOU FINISH BEFORE TIME IS CALLED, YOU MAY CHECK YOUR WORK ON THIS SECTION ONLY.
DO NOT WORK ON ANY OTHER SECTION IN THE TEST.

SECTION II

Time—35 minutes

25 Questions

Directions: The questions in this section are based on the reasoning contained in brief statements or passages. For some questions, more than one of the choices could conceivably answer the question. However, you are to choose the <u>best</u> answer; that is, the response that most accurately and completely answers the question. You should not make assumptions that are by commonsense standards implausible, superfluous, or incompatible with the passage. After you have chosen the best answer, blacken the corresponding space on your answer sheet.

1. Mayor: There has been a long debate in city council about how to accommodate projected increases in automobile traffic. Today, our choice is clear: either we adopt my plan to build a new expressway, or we do nothing. Doing nothing is not a viable option because our existing system of roads would be in gridlock within ten years given even a conservative estimate of future traffic levels. City council should therefore adopt my plan.

The reasoning in the mayor's argument is most vulnerable to which one of the following criticisms?

(A) It bases a projection only on conservative estimates rather than considering a wider range of estimates.

(B) It takes for granted that the options it considers are mutually exclusive.

(C) It fails to consider the possibility that the rate of increase in traffic will start to diminish after ten years.

(D) It fails to address the issue of the cost of traffic gridlock to the city's economy.

(E) It presents a choice that is limited to two options, without giving reasons for not considering any other options.

2. Museum curator: Our ancient Egyptian collection includes an earthenware hippopotamus that resembles a child's toy. It was discovered in a tomb, upside down, with its legs broken off. We know that the ancient Egyptians believed the dead had to wage eternal war with beasts. Breaking the legs off a representation of an animal was thought to help a deceased person in this war. We conclude that, far from being a toy, this hippopotamus was a religious object.

Which one of the following is an assumption required by the curator's argument?

(A) The tomb in which the hippopotamus was found was not the tomb of a child.

(B) Earthenware figures were never used as children's toys in ancient Egypt.

(C) The tomb in which the hippopotamus was found was not reentered from the time of burial until archaeologists opened it.

(D) The hippopotamus' legs were not broken through some natural occurrence after it was placed in the tomb.

(E) The hippopotamus was originally placed upside down in the tomb.

GO ON TO THE NEXT PAGE.

3. Lawyer: Juries are traditionally given their instructions in convoluted, legalistic language. The verbiage is intended to make the instructions more precise, but greater precision is of little use if most jurors have difficulty understanding the instructions. Since it is more important for jurors to have a basic but adequate understanding of their role than it is for the details of that role to be precisely specified, jury instructions should be formulated in simple, easily comprehensible language.

Each of the following, if true, strengthens the lawyer's argument EXCEPT:

(A) Most jurors are less likely to understand instructions given in convoluted, legalistic language than instructions given in simple, easily comprehensible language.

(B) Most jurors do not have an adequate understanding of their role after being given jury instructions in convoluted, legalistic language.

(C) Jury instructions formulated in simple, easily comprehensible language can adequately describe the role of the jurors.

(D) The details of the role of the jurors cannot be specified with complete precision in simple, easily comprehensible language.

(E) Jurors do not need to know the precise details of their role in order to have an adequate understanding of that role.

4. Traditional "talk" therapy, in which a patient with a psychological disorder discusses it with a trained therapist, produces chemical changes in the brain. These changes seem to correspond to improvements in certain aspects of the patient's behavior. Thus, physicians will eventually be able to treat such patients as effectively through pharmacological intervention in the brain's neurochemistry as through the lengthy intermediary of traditional "talk" methods.

Which one of the following is an assumption on which the argument depends?

(A) All neurochemical changes produce corresponding psychological changes.

(B) Improvements in a patient's behavior produced by "talk" therapy occur only through chemical changes in the brain's neurochemistry.

(C) "Talk" therapy has not been effective at bringing about psychological change.

(D) If chemical changes in the brain's neurochemistry correspond to improvements in patient behavior, then psychology and neuroscience will eventually be indistinguishable.

(E) Direct intervention in the brain's neurochemistry is likely to become a less expensive way of treating psychological disorders than is "talk" therapy.

5. Bacteria that benefit human beings when they are present in the body are called commensals. The bacterium *Helicobacter pylori* plays a primary role in the development of stomach ulcers. But since stomach ulcers occur in less than 10 percent of those harboring *H. pylori*, and since it allegedly strengthens immune response, many scientists now consider it a commensal. But this is surely misguided. Only about 10 percent of the people who harbor *Mycobacter tuberculosis*—a bacterium that can cause tuberculosis—get sick from it, yet no one would call *M. tuberculosis* a commensal.

Which one of the following, if true, most seriously undermines the argument's reasoning?

(A) Stomach ulcers caused by *H. pylori* and tuberculosis can both be effectively treated with antibiotics.

(B) Cases of tuberculosis usually last longer than ulcers caused by *H. pylori*.

(C) People who harbor *M. tuberculosis* derive no benefit from its presence.

(D) There are more people who harbor *M. tuberculosis* than people who harbor *H. pylori*.

(E) There are more people who harbor *H. pylori* than people who harbor *M. tuberculosis*.

6. Most apartments on the upper floors of The Vista Arms apartment building have scenic views. So there is in the building at least one studio apartment with scenic views.

The conclusion of the argument follows logically if which one of the following is assumed?

(A) All of the apartments on the lower floors of the building have scenic views.

(B) All of the apartments in the building have scenic views.

(C) Most of the apartments in the building are studio apartments.

(D) Most of the apartments with scenic views are on the upper floors of the building.

(E) Most of the apartments on the upper floors of the building are studio apartments.

GO ON TO THE NEXT PAGE.

7. Mike: Tom did not tell me that I could use his computer, but it would not be wrong for me to use it anyway. Last week Tom used Mary's bicycle even though she had not told him he could use it.

Which one of the following principles, if valid, would most help to justify Mike's reasoning?

(A) Using the possessions of others without their permission is not always theft.

(B) Generally one should tell the truth, but there are cases in which it is permissible not to.

(C) If people have used your property without your permission, it is not wrong for you to use their property without their permission.

(D) It is permissible to treat people in a way that is similar to the way in which they have treated others.

(E) Using another person's property is wrong if the person is harmed by that use.

8. Robinson: Wexell says that the museum wasted its money in purchasing props and costumes from famous stage productions, because such items have no artistic significance outside the context of a performance. But many of the props and costumes are too old and fragile for use in a performance. So clearly, the museum did not waste its money, for displaying these items is the only way of making them available to the public.

The reasoning in Robinson's argument is most vulnerable to criticism on the grounds that it

(A) offers anecdotal evidence insufficient to support a general claim

(B) gives reasons that do not address the point made in Wexell's argument

(C) attacks the person making the argument rather than the substance of the argument

(D) concludes that a claim is false merely on the grounds that the evidence for it is insufficient

(E) takes a condition that is sufficient for the conclusion to be true as one that is necessary for the conclusion to be true

9. In a party game, one person leaves the room with the understanding that someone else will relate a recent dream to the remaining group. The person then returns and tries to reconstruct the dream by asking only yes-or-no questions. In fact, no dream has been related: the group simply answers the questions according to some arbitrary rule. Surprisingly, the person usually constructs a dream narrative that is both coherent and ingenious.

The example presented above most closely conforms to which one of the following propositions?

(A) The presumption that something has order and coherence can lead one to imbue it with order and coherence.

(B) One is less apt to reach a false understanding of what someone says than to make no sense out of it at all.

(C) Dreams are often just collections of images and ideas without coherent structures.

(D) Interpreting another person's dream requires that one understand the dream as a coherent narrative.

(E) People often invent clever and coherent stories to explain their behavior to other people.

10. Computer manufacturers have sought to make computer chips ever smaller, since decreasing the size of a computer's central processing unit (CPU) chip—without making that CPU chip any less sophisticated—will proportionally increase the speed of the CPU chip and the computer containing it. But since CPU chips cannot be made significantly smaller without decreasing their sophistication, computers cannot currently be made significantly faster.

Which one of the following is an assumption on which the argument depends?

(A) Computers cannot currently be made faster unless their CPU chips are made smaller.

(B) Even if CPU chips are made slightly less sophisticated, they cannot currently be made much smaller.

(C) If both the size and the sophistication of a CPU chip are decreased, the speed of that chip will decrease.

(D) Few, if any, computer manufacturers believe that computers can be made significantly faster.

(E) Increasing the sophistication of a CPU chip without increasing its size will proportionally increase its speed.

GO ON TO THE NEXT PAGE.

11. In the last year, biologists have learned that there are many more species of amphibians in existence than had previously been known. This definitely undermines environmentalists' claim that pollution is eliminating many of these species every year.

The reasoning in the argument above is most vulnerable to criticism on the grounds that it involves a confusion between

(A)   kinds of things and the things that are of those kinds
(B)   a condition necessary for a phenomenon and one that is sufficient for it
(C)   a cause and an effect
(D)   a correlation between two phenomena and a causal relationship between them
(E)   changes in our knowledge of objects and changes in the objects themselves

12. Because dried peat moss, which is derived from sphagnum moss, contains no chemical additives and is a renewable resource, many gardeners use large amounts of it as a soil conditioner in the belief that the practice is environmentally sound. They are mistaken. The millions of acres of sphagnum moss in the world contribute more oxygen to the atmosphere than do all of the world's rain forests combined, and the garden soil industry is depleting these areas much faster than they can renew themselves.

Which one of the following principles, if valid, most helps to justify the argument's reasoning?

(A)   Using a product may be environmentally unsound even if the product is a renewable resource and contains no chemical additive.
(B)   A practice is not environmentally sound if it significantly reduces the amount of oxygen entering the atmosphere.
(C)   A practice is environmentally sound if it helps to protect rain forests that contribute large amounts of oxygen to the atmosphere.
(D)   If the environmental benefits of a practice outweigh the environmental costs, that practice can be legitimately considered environmentally sound.
(E)   If the practices of an industry threaten a vital resource, those practices should be banned.

13. Brooks: I'm unhappy in my job, but I don't know whether I can accept the risks involved in quitting my job.

Morgenstern: The only risk in quitting is that of not finding another job. If you don't find one, you're going to be pretty unhappy. But you're already unhappy, so you might as well just quit.

Morgenstern's argument is flawed in that it

(A)   fails to take into account that unhappiness can vary in intensity or significance
(B)   relies on an assumption that is tantamount to assuming that the conclusion is true
(C)   mischaracterizes what Brooks says
(D)   conflates two different types of risk
(E)   reaches a generalization on the basis of a single case

14. Only Canadian films are shown at the Lac Nichoutec Film Festival. This year, most of the films that won prizes at that festival also won prizes at international film festivals.

If the above statements are true, which one of the following statements must also be true?

(A)   This year, most of the Canadian films that were shown at international film festivals won prizes at the Lac Nichoutec Film Festival.
(B)   Most of the Canadian films produced this year were shown at the Lac Nichoutec Film Festival.
(C)   Some of the films that won prizes at international film festivals this year were Canadian films.
(D)   This year, not every film that won a prize at the Lac Nichoutec Film Festival was also shown at an international film festival.
(E)   This year, at least one film that won a prize at an international film festival was not shown at the Lac Nichoutec Film Festival.

GO ON TO THE NEXT PAGE.

15. Commentator: Many social critics claim that contemporary journalists' cynical tendency to look for selfish motives behind the seemingly altruistic actions of powerful people undermines our society's well-being by convincing people that success is invariably associated with greed and mendacity. But the critics' claim is absurd. The cynicism of contemporary journalists cannot be a contributing factor to the undermining of our society's well-being, for journalists have always been cynics. Today's journalists are, if anything, more restrained than their predecessors.

The reasoning in the commentator's argument is most vulnerable to criticism on the grounds that it overlooks the possibility that

(A) widespread cynicism is beneficial to the well-being of society

(B) cynicism about the motives of powerful people increases with the amount of information one has about them

(C) the work of contemporary journalists reflects a cynicism that is not really genuine

(D) any accurate description of human behavior portrays it as selfish

(E) cynicism of this type on the part of journalists has always had a negative effect on the well-being of society

16. The owners of Uptown Apartments are leaning toward not improving the apartment complex; they believe that the increased rents they could charge for improved apartments would not cover the costs of the improvements. But the improvements would make the surrounding housing, which they also own, more valuable and rentable for higher rents. So the owners should make the improvements.

The reasoning in which one of the following is most similar to the reasoning in the argument above?

(A) John's injured knee does not cause him a lot of pain, so he does not want to undergo the pain of surgery to heal it. But the surgery would enable him to exercise regularly again. Thus John should have the surgery.

(B) Since its fishing season lasts only six months, Laketown Fishing Company prefers renting boats to buying its own. But since boats can be used for other purposes during the fishing season, it has made the wrong decision.

(C) Max's mechanic thinks there is a crack in the left cylinder head of Max's car and wants to remove the engine to check. Such a diagnostic engine removal would cost about $175, even if the cylinder head does not need replacement. But if the cylinder head is cracked and is not replaced, the engine will be ruined. So Max should have the mechanic check for the crack.

(D) Because of dental problems, Leona cut her consumption of candy. Consequently, she learned to enjoy fruit more. Thus, dental problems, which can lead to other health problems, led in her case to an improved diet and better health overall.

(E) Bulk Fruit Company is deciding whether to market a new hybrid fruit. It is enthusiastic about the idea, since research suggests that people will come to like this fruit. Therefore, it is in the long-term interest of the company to market the hybrid fruit.

GO ON TO THE NEXT PAGE.

17. Ditalgame Corporation's computer video games are subject to widespread illegal copying. To combat this piracy, Ditalgame will begin using a new copy protection feature on its games. Ditalgame's president predicts a substantial increase in sales of the company's games once the new copy protection feature is implemented.

Which one of the following, if true, provides the most support for the president's prediction?

(A) Ditalgame has spent millions of dollars developing the new copy protection feature, and the company can recoup these costs only if its sales increase substantially.

(B) Over the last several years, the market for computer games has grown steadily, but Ditalgame's share of that market has shrunk considerably.

(C) The copy protection feature causes a copied game to be playable just long enough for most people to come to enjoy it so much that they decide they have to have it.

(D) *Game Review Monthly*, the most commonly read magazine among people who frequently copy computer games, generally gives favorable reviews to Ditalgame games.

(E) Computer games produced by Ditalgame are copied more frequently than computer games produced by Ditalgame's main competitors.

18. Columnist: It may soon be possible for an economy to function without paper money. Instead, the government would electronically record all transactions as they take place. However, while this may be technologically feasible it would never be willingly accepted by a society, for it gives the government too much power. People are rightly distrustful of governments with too much power.

Which one of the following most accurately expresses the overall conclusion of the columnist's argument?

(A) A society would never willingly accept a system in which, in lieu of paper money, the government keeps track of every transaction electronically.

(B) It is reasonable for people to distrust a government that has too much power.

(C) New technology may soon make it possible for an economy to operate without paper money.

(D) People are right to be unwilling to give the government the power it would need to operate an economy without paper money.

(E) Even though it may be technologically feasible, no government will be able to operate an economy without the use of paper money.

19. Social scientist: Since the body of thought known as Marxism claims to describe rigorously an inexorable historical movement toward the socialization of the means of production, it should be regarded as a scientific theory. Thus, certain interpreters, in taking Marxism as a political program aimed at radically transforming society, have misconstrued it.

The social scientist's conclusion follows logically if which one of the following is assumed?

(A) The description that Marxism gives of certain historical phenomena in the economic sphere is as rigorous as it is claimed to be.

(B) The aims of science are incompatible with the aims of those who would seek to transform society by political means.

(C) Only bodies of thought consisting purely of rigorous description are scientific theories.

(D) Scientific theories cannot be correctly interpreted to be, or to imply, political programs.

(E) The means of production will inevitably become socialized regardless of any political programs designed to make that occur.

20. Daniel: There are certain actions that moral duty obliges us to perform regardless of their consequences. However, an action is not morally good simply because it fulfills a moral obligation. No action can be morally good unless it is performed with the right motivations.

Carrie: Our motivations for our actions are not subject to our conscious control. Therefore, the only thing that can be required for an action to be morally good is that it fulfill a moral obligation.

The dialogue most supports the claim that Daniel and Carrie are committed to disagreeing with each other about the truth of which one of the following statements?

(A) No one can be morally required to do something that is impossible to do.

(B) Some actions that are performed with the right motivations are not morally good.

(C) All actions that fulfill moral obligations are performed in order to fulfill moral obligations.

(D) An action performed with the wrong motivations cannot be morally good.

(E) If a person's motivations for acting are based on a sense of duty, then that person's action is morally good.

GO ON TO THE NEXT PAGE.

21. The mayor was not telling the truth when he said that the bridge renovation did not waste taxpayers' money. The very commission he set up to look into government waste reported that the Southern Tier Project, of which the bridge renovation was a part, was egregiously wasteful.

The reasoning in the argument is flawed in that the argument

(A) infers that a part has a certain quality merely on the grounds that the whole to which it belongs has that quality

(B) draws a general conclusion about government waste on the basis of a single instance of such waste

(C) attacks the mayor's character rather than assessing the strength of the evidence supporting the mayor's claim

(D) puts forward evidence that presupposes an important part of the claim that the argument attempts to support

(E) rejects a position on the grounds that the motives of the person who has advanced the position were not disinterested

22. The airport's runways are too close to each other to allow simultaneous use of adjacent runways when visibility is poor, so the airport allows only 30 planes an hour to land in poor weather; in good weather 60 planes an hour are allowed to land. Because airline schedules assume good weather, bad weather creates serious delays.

Which one of the following is most strongly supported by the information above?

(A) In poor weather, only half as many planes are allowed to land each hour on any one runway at the airport as are allowed to land on it in good weather.

(B) When the weather at the airport is good it is likely that there are planes landing on two adjacent runways at any given time.

(C) If any two of the airport's runways are used simultaneously, serious delays result.

(D) Airlines using the airport base their schedules on the assumption that more than 30 planes an hour will be allowed to land at the airport.

(E) In good weather, there are few if any seriously delayed flights at the airport.

23. As a general rule, the larger a social group of primates, the more time its members spend grooming one another. The main purpose of this social grooming is the maintenance of social cohesion. Furthermore, group size among primates tends to increase proportionally with the size of the neocortex, the seat of higher thought in the brain. Extrapolating upon the relationship between group size and neocortex size, we can infer that early human groups were quite large. But unexpectedly, there is strong evidence that, apart from parents grooming their children, these humans spent virtually no time grooming one another.

Which one of the following, if true, would do most to resolve the apparent discrepancy described above?

(A) Early humans were much more likely to groom themselves than are the members of other primate species.

(B) Early humans developed languages, which provided a more effective way of maintaining social cohesion than social grooming.

(C) Early humans were not as extensively covered with hair as are other primates, and consequently they had less need for social grooming.

(D) While early humans probably lived in large groups, there is strong evidence that they hunted in small groups.

(E) Many types of primates other than humans have fairly large neocortex regions and display frequent social grooming.

GO ON TO THE NEXT PAGE.

24. Had the party's economic theories been sound and had it succeeded in implementing its program, the inflation rate would have lessened considerably. But because the inflation rate actually increased, the party's economic theories were far off the mark.

The flawed reasoning in which one of the following arguments most closely resembles the flawed reasoning in the argument above?

(A) If the people who inhabited the valley for so long had been invaded, or if there had been a dramatic climatic change, there would have been changes in the valley's architecture. But architecture in the valley remained the same throughout their stay. Thus, the valley people must not have been invaded at any time during their stay.

(B) Many people fear that if the opposition party wins the election and keeps its promise to cut wages dramatically, workers in key industries will strike. But because the workers have promised not to strike, these workers must think the party will not keep its promise of a dramatic wage cut.

(C) If the company had succeeded in selling its subsidiaries and used the cash to purchase the new patent, its stock price would have doubled in the last two years. But the price of the stock did not increase in that time. Thus, the company must have failed to sell its subsidiaries.

(D) City residents were expected to show a great deal of support for the rebels if the battle was won and the jailed rebel leaders freed. Residents have shown a great deal of support for the rebels for the last three days. Therefore, the rebels must have won the battle.

(E) If the television station's new weather forecasting equipment had been worth the investment, the accuracy of its forecasts would have risen, along with its ratings. But the station's ratings actually decreased. Thus, the new equipment is no improvement on the old.

25. When a group is unable to reach a consensus, group members are often accused of being stubborn, bull-headed, or unyielding. Such epithets often seem abusive, are difficult to prove, and rarely help the group reach a resolution. Those who wish to make such an accusation stick, however, should choose "unyielding," because one can always appeal to the fact that the accused has not yielded; obviously if one acknowledges that a person has not yielded, then one cannot deny that the person is unyielding, at least on this issue.

Which one of the following most accurately describes the argumentative technique employed above?

(A) rejecting a tactic on the grounds that it constitutes an attack on the character of a person and has no substance in fact

(B) rejecting a tactic on the grounds that the tactic makes it virtually impossible for the group to reach a consensus on the issue in question

(C) conditionally advocating a tactic on the grounds that it results in an accusation that is less offensive than the alternatives

(D) conditionally advocating a tactic on the grounds that it results in an argument that would help the group to reach a consensus on the issue in question

(E) conditionally advocating a tactic on the grounds that it results in an argument for which one could not consistently accept the premise but deny the conclusion

S T O P

IF YOU FINISH BEFORE TIME IS CALLED, YOU MAY CHECK YOUR WORK ON THIS SECTION ONLY.
DO NOT WORK ON ANY OTHER SECTION IN THE TEST.

SECTION III

Time—35 minutes

23 Questions

Directions: Each group of questions in this section is based on a set of conditions. In answering some of the questions, it may be useful to draw a rough diagram. Choose the response that most accurately and completely answers each question and blacken the corresponding space on your answer sheet.

Questions 1–5

A chemistry class has six lab sessions scheduled over three days—Wednesday, Thursday, and Friday—one session being held each morning and one each afternoon. Each session will be led by a different lab assistant—Julio, Kevin, Lan, Nessa, Olivia, or Rebecca. The assignment of lab assistants to sessions is constrained as follows:

    Kevin and Rebecca must lead sessions that meet on the same day.

    Lan and Olivia cannot lead sessions that meet on the same day.

    Nessa must lead an afternoon session.

    Julio's session must meet on an earlier day of the week than Olivia's.

1. Which one of the following could be an accurate assignment of lab assistants to morning and afternoon sessions, respectively, on the three days?

(A)   Wednesday: Rebecca, Kevin
        Thursday: Julio, Lan
        Friday: Nessa, Olivia

(B)   Wednesday: Olivia, Nessa
        Thursday: Julio, Lan
        Friday: Kevin, Rebecca

(C)   Wednesday: Lan, Kevin
        Thursday: Rebecca, Julio
        Friday: Olivia, Nessa

(D)   Wednesday: Kevin, Rebecca
        Thursday: Julio, Nessa
        Friday: Olivia, Lan

(E)   Wednesday: Julio, Lan
        Thursday: Olivia, Nessa
        Friday: Rebecca, Kevin

GO ON TO THE NEXT PAGE.

2. If Lan does not lead a Wednesday session, then which one of the following lab assistants must lead a Thursday session?

    (A) Rebecca
    (B) Olivia
    (C) Nessa
    (D) Kevin
    (E) Julio

3. If Kevin's session meets on the day before Nessa's, then which one of the following is a complete and accurate list of lab assistants any one of whom could lead the Thursday afternoon session?

    (A) Julio, Nessa
    (B) Kevin, Rebecca
    (C) Kevin, Nessa, Rebecca
    (D) Julio, Kevin, Nessa, Rebecca
    (E) Julio, Kevin, Lan, Nessa, Rebecca

4. If Julio and Kevin both lead morning sessions, then any of the following could be true EXCEPT:

    (A) Lan's session meets Wednesday morning.
    (B) Lan's session meets Thursday afternoon.
    (C) Nessa's session meets Friday afternoon.
    (D) Olivia's session meets Thursday morning.
    (E) Olivia's session meets Friday morning.

5. If Julio leads the Thursday afternoon session, then for how many of the other lab assistants can one determine which sessions they lead?

    (A) one
    (B) two
    (C) three
    (D) four
    (E) five

GO ON TO THE NEXT PAGE.

Questions 6–11

A shopping center has exactly seven spaces—space 1 through space 7—arranged in a straight row. Seven businesses—an optometrist, a pharmacy, two restaurants, a shoe store, a toy store, and a veterinarian—will be located in the shopping center, one in each space. The locations of the businesses are subject to the following constraints:

    The pharmacy must be at one end of the row and one of the restaurants at the other.

    The two restaurants must be separated by at least two other businesses.

    The pharmacy must be next to either the optometrist or the veterinarian.

    The toy store cannot be next to the veterinarian.

6. Which one of the following could be the order of the businesses in spaces 1 through 7 respectively?

    (A)   pharmacy, optometrist, shoe store, restaurant, veterinarian, toy store, restaurant

    (B)   pharmacy, veterinarian, optometrist, shoe store, restaurant, toy store, restaurant

    (C)   restaurant, shoe store, veterinarian, pharmacy, optometrist, toy store, restaurant

    (D)   restaurant, toy store, optometrist, restaurant, veterinarian, shoe store, pharmacy

    (E)   restaurant, optometrist, toy store, restaurant, shoe store, veterinarian, pharmacy

GO ON TO THE NEXT PAGE.

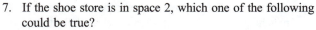

7. If the shoe store is in space 2, which one of the following could be true?

(A)   The optometrist is in space 5.
(B)   The pharmacy is in space 1.
(C)   A restaurant is in space 3.
(D)   The toy store is in space 6.
(E)   The veterinarian is in space 4.

8. If the veterinarian is in space 5, which one of the following must be true?

(A)   The optometrist is in space 2.
(B)   The pharmacy is in space 7.
(C)   A restaurant is in space 4.
(D)   The shoe store is in space 6.
(E)   The toy store is in space 3.

9. If the optometrist is next to the shoe store, the businesses immediately on either side of this pair must be

(A)   the pharmacy and a restaurant
(B)   the pharmacy and the toy store
(C)   the two restaurants
(D)   a restaurant and the toy store
(E)   a restaurant and the veterinarian

10. If the shoe store is in space 4, which one of the following must be true?

(A)   The optometrist is next to a restaurant.
(B)   The pharmacy is next to the veterinarian.
(C)   A restaurant is next to the toy store.
(D)   The shoe store is next to the toy store.
(E)   The shoe store is next to the veterinarian.

11. Which one of the following, if substituted for the constraint that the two restaurants must be separated by at least two other businesses, would have the same effect in determining the locations of the businesses?

(A)   A restaurant must be in either space 3, space 4, or space 5.
(B)   A restaurant must be next to either the optometrist or the veterinarian.
(C)   Either the toy store or the veterinarian must be somewhere between the two restaurants.
(D)   No more than two businesses can separate the pharmacy and the restaurant nearest it.
(E)   The optometrist cannot be next to the shoe store.

GO ON TO THE NEXT PAGE.

Questions 12–18

A software company employs exactly seven sales representatives—Kim, Mahr, Parra, Quinn, Stuckey, Tiao, and Udall—to work in its three sales zones—Zone 1, Zone 2, and Zone 3. Each sales representative works in exactly one of the sales zones, in accordance with the following conditions:

Either Parra or Tiao (but not both) works in Zone 1.
Either Tiao or Udall (but not both) works in Zone 2.
Parra and Quinn work in the same sales zone as each other.
Stuckey and Udall work in the same sales zone as each other.
There are more of the sales representatives working in Zone 3 than in Zone 2.

12. Which one of the following could be an accurate matching of the sales representatives to the sales zones in which they work?

(A)   Zone 1: Kim, Parra
       Zone 2: Stuckey, Udall
       Zone 3: Mahr, Quinn, Tiao
(B)   Zone 1: Kim, Tiao
       Zone 2: Stuckey, Udall
       Zone 3: Mahr, Parra, Quinn
(C)   Zone 1: Parra, Quinn
       Zone 2: Kim, Udall
       Zone 3: Mahr, Stuckey, Tiao
(D)   Zone 1: Stuckey, Udall
       Zone 2: Kim, Tiao
       Zone 3: Mahr, Parra, Quinn
(E)   Zone 1: Tiao
       Zone 2: Kim, Parra, Quinn
       Zone 3: Stuckey, Udall

GO ON TO THE NEXT PAGE.

13. If more sales representatives work in Zone 1 than in Zone 3, then which one of the following could be true?

   (A) Kim works in Zone 2.
   (B) Mahr works in Zone 2.
   (C) Parra works in Zone 3.
   (D) Tiao works in Zone 1.
   (E) Udall works in Zone 3.

14. Which one of the following must be false?

   (A) Kim and Stuckey both work in Zone 1.
   (B) Kim and Stuckey both work in Zone 3.
   (C) Mahr and Stuckey both work in Zone 3.
   (D) Mahr and Udall both work in Zone 3.
   (E) Parra and Stuckey both work in Zone 1.

15. Which one of the following could be a complete and accurate list of the sales representatives working in Zone 3?

   (A) Kim, Mahr
   (B) Kim, Tiao
   (C) Parra, Quinn
   (D) Stuckey, Tiao, Udall
   (E) Parra, Quinn, Stuckey, Udall

16. Quinn CANNOT work in the same sales zone as which one of the following?

   (A) Kim
   (B) Mahr
   (C) Stuckey
   (D) Tiao
   (E) Udall

17. Item Removed From Scoring.

18. If Mahr and Stuckey work in the same sales zone, then which one of the following could be true?

   (A) Kim works in Zone 2.
   (B) Mahr works in Zone 1.
   (C) Parra works in Zone 3.
   (D) Stuckey works in Zone 2.
   (E) Tiao works in Zone 1.

GO ON TO THE NEXT PAGE.

Questions 19–23

During a recital, two pianists—Wayne and Zara—will perform solos. There will be five solos altogether, performed one immediately after another. Each solo will be either a modern piece or a traditional piece. The choice of pianist and type of piece for the solos must conform to the following conditions:

The third solo is a traditional piece.

Exactly two of the traditional pieces are performed consecutively.

In the fourth solo, either Wayne performs a traditional piece or Zara performs a modern piece.

The pianist who performs the second solo does not perform the fifth solo.

No traditional piece is performed until Wayne performs at least one modern piece.

19. Which one of the following could be all of the solos that are traditional pieces?

(A) the first, third, and fourth
(B) the second, third, and fourth
(C) the third and fourth
(D) the third and fifth
(E) the fourth and fifth

GO ON TO THE NEXT PAGE.

20. What is the minimum number of solos in which Wayne performs a traditional piece?

   (A)   zero
   (B)   one
   (C)   two
   (D)   three
   (E)   four

21. If the pianist who performs the first solo also performs the second solo, then which one of the following must be true?

   (A)   Zara performs the first solo.
   (B)   Wayne performs the third solo.
   (C)   Zara performs the fifth solo.
   (D)   The second solo is a traditional piece.
   (E)   The fourth solo is a modern piece.

22. If the fifth solo is a traditional piece, then for exactly how many of the solos is the choice of pianist completely determined?

   (A)   one
   (B)   two
   (C)   three
   (D)   four
   (E)   five

23. If in the fifth solo Wayne performs a traditional piece, which one of the following could be true?

   (A)   Zara performs the first solo.
   (B)   Wayne performs the second solo.
   (C)   Zara performs the third solo.
   (D)   The second solo is a modern piece.
   (E)   The fourth solo is a traditional piece.

S T O P

IF YOU FINISH BEFORE TIME IS CALLED, YOU MAY CHECK YOUR WORK ON THIS SECTION ONLY.
DO NOT WORK ON ANY OTHER SECTION IN THE TEST.

SECTION IV

Time—35 minutes

26 Questions

<u>Directions:</u> The questions in this section are based on the reasoning contained in brief statements or passages. For some questions, more than one of the choices could conceivably answer the question. However, you are to choose the <u>best</u> answer; that is, the response that most accurately and completely answers the question. You should not make assumptions that are by commonsense standards implausible, superfluous, or incompatible with the passage. After you have chosen the best answer, blacken the corresponding space on your answer sheet.

1. According to the official results of last week's national referendum, 80 percent voted in favor of the proposal. But those results must be rigged. Everyone I know voted against the proposal, which is clear evidence that most people voted against it.

Which one of the following most accurately describes a flaw in the reasoning of the argument?

(A) The argument uses evidence drawn from a sample that is unlikely to be representative of the general population.
(B) The argument presumes the truth of the conclusion that it sets out to prove.
(C) The argument rejects a claim by attacking the proponents of the claim rather than addressing the claim itself.
(D) The argument fails to make a needed distinction between how people should have voted and how they actually voted.
(E) The argument defends a claim solely on the grounds that most people believe it.

2. Editorial: It is usually desirable for people to have access to unregulated information, such as is found on the Internet. But a vast array of misinformation will always show up on the Internet, and it is difficult to determine which information is accurate. Accurate information is useless unless it can easily be distinguished from misinformation; thus, the information on the Internet should somehow be regulated.

Which one of the following principles, if valid, most helps to justify the editorial's argument?

(A) It is never possible to regulate misinformation without restricting people's access to accurate information.
(B) Even if information is regulated, accurate information is often indistinguishable from misinformation.
(C) Regulation of information makes it easy for people to distinguish between accurate information and misinformation.
(D) It is acceptable for people to have access to a vast array of misinformation only if accurate information is never overlooked as a result.
(E) It is usually more desirable for people to have access to useless, unregulated misinformation than it is for them to have access only to accurate but regulated information.

3. Some members have criticized the club's president for inviting Dr. Hines to speak at the annual awards banquet without consulting other club members beforehand. But a few years ago the previous club president hired a tax accountant even though he had not discussed it with club members beforehand. So the current president acted appropriately in the way in which she invited Dr. Hines.

Which one of the following is an assumption on which the argument relies?

(A) The previous club president had also invited speakers without first consulting other club members.
(B) At the time the previous club president hired the tax accountant, most club members did not expect to be consulted about such matters.
(C) Dr. Hines accepted the president's invitation to speak at the club's annual awards banquet.
(D) The club president has more discretion in hiring an accountant than in hiring a speaker.
(E) The club's previous president acted appropriately in hiring the tax accountant without first consulting other club members.

4. Company spokesperson: *Household Products* magazine claims that our Filterator X water filter does not remove chemical contaminants in significant amounts. This attack on the quality of our product is undermined by the experience of the millions of Filterator X owners who are satisfied with the product's performance.

Which one of the following, if true, most seriously undermines the company spokesperson's argument?

(A) *Household Products* did not evaluate whether the Filterator X water filter significantly improved the taste of drinking water.
(B) Most Filterator X owners have no way to determine how effectively the product removes chemical contaminants from water.
(C) People whose household water contains chemical contaminants are more likely than other people to buy a Filterator X water filter.
(D) Very few people who own a Filterator X read *Household Products* on a consistent basis.
(E) *Household Products*' evaluations of Filterator X water filters have been consistently negative.

GO ON TO THE NEXT PAGE.

5. A famous artist once claimed that all great art imitates nature. If this claim is correct, then any music that is great art would imitate nature. But while some music may imitate ocean waves or the galloping of horses, for example, most great music imitates nothing at all.

Which one of the following most accurately expresses the main point of the argument?

(A)   Music is inferior to the other arts.
(B)   Either the artist's claim is incorrect, or most great music is not great art.
(C)   Like some great music, some great painting and sculpture may fail to imitate nature.
(D)   Some elements of nature cannot be represented adequately by great art.
(E)   Sounds that do not imitate nature are not great music.

6. Patricia: During Japan's Tokugawa period, martial arts experts known as ninjas were trained for the purposes of espionage and assassination. Yet at that time there was actually very little ninja activity in Japan, and most Japanese did not fear ninjas.

Tamara: That is not true. Many wealthy Japanese during the Tokugawa period had their houses constructed with intentionally squeaky floors so that they would receive warning if a ninja were in the house.

Of the following, which one, if true, is the strongest counter Patricia can make to Tamara's objection?

(A)   Many poor Japanese during the Tokugawa period also had houses constructed with intentionally squeaky floors.
(B)   As part of their secret training, ninjas learned to walk on squeaky floors without making a sound.
(C)   The wealthy made up a small portion of Japan's population during the Tokugawa period.
(D)   The fighting prowess of ninjas was exaggerated to mythic proportions in the years following the Tokugawa period.
(E)   There were very few ninjas at any time other than during the Tokugawa period.

7. Philosopher: Both the consequences and the motives of human actions have bearing on the moral worth of those actions. Nonetheless, to be a moral agent one must have free will, because one cannot be a moral agent without desiring to conform to a principle.

The philosopher's argument requires the assumption that

(A)   one cannot be a moral agent if one lacks a concern for the consequences of actions
(B)   desiring to conform to a principle requires free will
(C)   nobody who acts without taking the consequences of the action into consideration is free
(D)   it is impossible to have desires without also being a moral agent
(E)   it is impossible to perform morally worthy actions without at some time conforming to a principle

8. A significant amount of the acquisition budget of a typical university library is spent on subscriptions to scholarly journals. Over the last several years, the average subscription rate a library pays for such a journal has increased dramatically, even though the costs of publishing a scholarly journal have remained fairly constant. Obviously, then, in most cases publishing a scholarly journal must be much more profitable now than it was several years ago.

Which one of the following, if true, most seriously weakens the argument?

(A)   Many university libraries have begun to charge higher and higher fines for overdue books and periodicals as a way of passing on increased journal subscription costs to library users.
(B)   A university library's acquisition budget usually represents only a small fraction of its total operating budget.
(C)   Publishing a scholarly journal is an expensive enterprise, and publishers of such journals cannot survive financially if they consistently lose money.
(D)   Most subscribers to scholarly journals are individuals, not libraries, and the subscription rates for individuals have generally remained unchanged for the past several years.
(E)   The majority of scholarly journals are published no more than four times a year.

GO ON TO THE NEXT PAGE.

9. Terrence Gurney suggests that because his books appeal to a wide audience, he is not given due credit for his literary achievements. Surely he is mistaken. Gurney's books tell interesting stories, but the writing is flat, leaving no lasting impression on the reader. This is likely the reason that Gurney has not received praise for literary achievement.

Which one of the following most accurately states the argument's overall conclusion?

(A) Terrence Gurney is mistaken when he suggests that the wide appeal of his books has prevented him from being given due credit for his literary achievements.
(B) Terrence Gurney's books are not significant literary achievements.
(C) Even though Terrence Gurney's books tell interesting stories, his writing is flat and leaves no lasting impression on the reader.
(D) Terrence Gurney has not been given due credit for his literary achievements because his books appeal to such a wide audience.
(E) Terrence Gurney should have received some praise for his literary achievements despite the fact that his writing is flat and leaves no lasting impression on the reader.

10. In an experiment designed to show how life may have begun on Earth, scientists demonstrated that an electrical spark—or lightning—could produce amino acids, the building blocks of Earth's life. However, unless the spark occurs in a "reducing" atmosphere, that is, one rich in hydrogen and lean in oxygen, amino acids do not form readily and tend to break apart when they do form. Scientists now believe that Earth's atmosphere was actually rich in oxygen and lean in nitrogen at the time life began.

Assuming that the scientists' current belief about Earth's atmosphere at the time life began is correct, which one of the following, if true, would most help to explain how lightning could have produced the first amino acids on Earth?

(A) Meteorite impacts at the time life began on Earth temporarily created a reducing atmosphere around the impact site.
(B) A single amino acid could have been sufficient to begin the formation of life on Earth.
(C) Earth's atmosphere has changed significantly since life first began.
(D) Lightning was less common on Earth at the time life began than it is now.
(E) Asteroids contain amino acids, and some of these amino acids could survive an asteroid's impact with Earth.

11. Art critic: The Woerner Journalism Award for criticism was given to Nan Paulsen for her reviews of automobiles. This is inappropriate. The criticism award should be given for criticism, which Paulsen's reviews clearly were not. After all, cars are utilitarian things, not works of art. And objects that are not works of art do not reveal important truths about the culture that produced them.

Which one of the following principles, if valid, most helps to justify the reasoning in the art critic's argument?

(A) The Woerner Journalism Award for criticism should not be given to a writer who portrays utilitarian objects as works of art.
(B) Reviews of objects cannot appropriately be considered to be criticism unless the objects reveal important truths about the culture that produced them.
(C) Unless a review is written for the purpose of revealing important truths about the writer's culture, that review should not be considered to be criticism.
(D) The Woerner Journalism Award for criticism should not be given to writers who do not consider themselves to be critics.
(E) All writing that reveals important truths about a culture should be considered to be criticism.

12. Manager: Our company's mail-order sales have recently increased 25 percent. This increase started around the time we started offering unlimited free shipping, rather than just free shipping on orders over $50. Thus, our change in policy probably caused the increase.

Which one of the following, if true, most strengthens the manager's argument?

(A) Mail-order sales have been decreasing for companies that do not offer unlimited free shipping.
(B) The company did not widely advertise its change in policy.
(C) The company's profits from mail-order sales have increased since the change in policy.
(D) The company's change in policy occurred well after its competitors started offering unlimited free shipping.
(E) Most companies offer free shipping only on mail-order purchases over $50.

GO ON TO THE NEXT PAGE.

13. Proponents of nuclear power point out that new nuclear plants are so technologically sophisticated that the chances of a meltdown are extremely small. This is true, but it would still be unwise to build nuclear power plants, since the consequences of a meltdown are absolutely catastrophic.

The pattern of reasoning in which one of the following is most similar to that in the argument above?

(A) Many mountain climbers claim that their sport is safe because mishaps, though often fatal, are rare. However, mountain climbing is very risky: although the number of mishaps is small, so is the number of mountain climbers. Hence, the chance of a fatal mishap during mountain climbing is not as slim as it may seem.

(B) Eating a serving of vegetables just once will not improve your health. It is nonetheless prudent to do so, for eating vegetables every day will make you much healthier over time.

(C) Skydivers always use two parachutes: a main chute and an auxiliary one in case the main chute malfunctions. Thus, the risk of a fatal mishap is low. Nonetheless, it is foolish to skydive, for though the risk is small, the rewards from skydiving are also small.

(D) The risk of serious injury when bungee jumping is quite low. Nonetheless, it is reckless to engage in that activity, for the injuries that would result in the case of an accident are so extreme that it is not worth the risk.

(E) People complain about having to wear seat belts because they believe the chances of traffic accidents are slim. This is true; on any given trip it is unlikely that a collision will occur. However, it is still unwise to ride in a car without a seat belt, for the effort it takes to put one on is minimal.

14. University president: Research institutions have an obligation to promote research in any field of theoretical investigation if that research shows some promise of yielding insights into the causes of practical problems that affect people's quality of life.

The principle stated by the university president, if valid, most helps to justify which one of the following actions?

(A) A university denies a grant application from a faculty member for work on a solution to a famous mathematical puzzle that has no relation to practical concerns.

(B) A government agency funds a research project in astrophysics designed to determine whether there are theoretical limits on the magnitude of planets in distant solar systems.

(C) A university funds a research position in the physics department that involves no teaching but has the responsibility for managing all the grant applications by members of the physics faculty.

(D) A foundation decides not to fund a research proposal in applied mathematics that sought to model certain poorly understood aspects of economic behavior.

(E) A research institute funds an investigation into the mathematical properties of folded structures that is likely to aid in understanding the structure of proteins that cause disease.

GO ON TO THE NEXT PAGE.

15. Carpal tunnel syndrome, a nerve disorder that affects the hands and wrists, is often caused by repetitive motions such as typing on a keyboard. A recent study of office workers found that, among those who do similar amounts of typing, workers reporting the least control over their own work had almost three times the risk of developing carpal tunnel syndrome as did those who reported the most control.

Which one of the following, if true, most helps to explain the study's findings?

(A) Office workers who have the most control over their own work tend to do significantly less typing than do those who have the least control over their own work.

(B) Feeling a lack of control over one's own work tends to put one under emotional stress that makes one more susceptible to nerve disorders.

(C) The keyboards on which office workers type tend to put typists' arms and hands in positions that promote the development of carpal tunnel syndrome.

(D) Among office workers who rarely use keyboards, the rate of carpal tunnel syndrome is much higher for those who feel that they lack control over their own work.

(E) Office workers who have the most control over their own work tend to perform repetitive motions other than typing more often than do office workers with the least control over their own work.

16. Principle: Employees of telemarketing agencies should never do anything that predisposes people to dislike the agencies' clients.

Application: If an employee of a telemarketing agency has been told by a person the employee has called that he or she does not want to buy the product of a client of the agency, the employee should not try to talk that person into doing so.

Which one of the following, if true, justifies the given application of the principle above?

(A) Any employee of a telemarketing agency is likely to be able to determine whether trying to talk someone into buying the product of a client of the agency after the person has said that he or she does not want to will likely engender animosity toward the client.

(B) Some employees of telemarketing agencies are unlikely to be certain about whether trying to talk someone into buying the product of a client of the agency after the person has said that he or she does not want to will likely engender animosity toward the client.

(C) Any employee of a telemarketing agency who tries to get someone to buy the product of a client of the agency after the person has said that he or she does not want to will engender animosity toward the client.

(D) Some people that an employee of a telemarketing agency calls to ask them to buy the product of a client of the agency will refuse to do so even though they are not predisposed to dislike the client.

(E) People who are already predisposed to dislike the client of a telemarketing agency are more likely to refuse to buy the product of that client than are people who are predisposed to like the client.

GO ON TO THE NEXT PAGE.

17. Although Pluto has an atmosphere and is much larger than any asteroid, Pluto is not a true planet. Pluto formed in orbit around the planet Neptune and was then ejected from orbit around Neptune when Triton, Neptune's largest moon, was captured by Neptune's gravity.

The conclusion of the argument follows logically if which one of the following is assumed?

(A) No celestial body can simultaneously be a moon and a planet.
(B) Not all celestial bodies that have an atmosphere and orbit the sun are true planets.
(C) If Pluto had not been ejected from its orbit around Neptune, Pluto would not have its current orbit around the sun and would still be a moon.
(D) The size of a celestial body in orbit around the sun is not relevant to determining whether or not it is a true planet.
(E) For a celestial body to be a true planet it must have formed in orbit around the sun exclusively.

18. A high-calorie diet providing adequate fats was a crucial requirement for the evolution of the anatomically modern human brain, a process that began among our early human ancestors. Food resources that could support such a diet were most abundant and reliable in the shore environments that were available to early humans. Nevertheless, the human brain's evolution took place almost exclusively in savanna and woodland areas.

Which one of the following, if true, would most help to resolve the apparent conflict presented above?

(A) Early humans had a significantly lower metabolic rate than anatomically modern humans, allowing them to expend their fat reserves more efficiently.
(B) The brains of the earliest known humans were 30 percent smaller than the anatomically modern human brain.
(C) Prehistoric savanna and woodland areas offered more reliable and abundant resources than they do today.
(D) The techniques used to explore the archaeology of prehistoric shore sites have only recently been developed.
(E) Gathering food in shore environments required a significantly greater expenditure of calories by early humans than did gathering food in other environments.

19. Editor Y: This is a good photograph: the composition is attractive, especially in the way the image is blurred by smoke in one corner.

Editor Z: It's very pretty, but it's a bad photograph. It doesn't make a statement; there's no obvious reason for the smoke to be there.

The editors' dialogue provides the most support for the claim that they disagree with each other about whether

(A) a photograph's composition should be related to a statement that it makes
(B) a photograph that is not attractive can still be a good photograph
(C) a photograph that makes no statement can still be attractive
(D) attractiveness by itself can make a photograph a good photograph
(E) attractive composition and prettiness are the same feature

20. University president: We will be forced to reduce spending next year if we do not increase our enrollment. So, if we are to maintain the quality of the education we provide, we must market our programs more aggressively. Without such marketing we will be unable to increase our enrollment.

The conclusion of the university president's argument can be properly drawn if which one of the following is assumed?

(A) The university will not maintain the quality of the education it provides if it increases its enrollment.
(B) The university will not need to reduce spending next year if it increases its enrollment.
(C) The university will increase its enrollment if it markets its programs more aggressively.
(D) The university will not maintain the quality of the education it provides if it reduces spending next year.
(E) The university will not need to reduce spending next year if it markets its programs more aggressively.

GO ON TO THE NEXT PAGE.

21. If the city starts requiring residents to sort the materials that they put out for recycling, then many residents will put more recyclables in with their regular garbage. This will result in more recyclables being buried in the city's landfill. However, because of the cost of having city workers do the sorting, the sanitation department will not stay within its budget unless the sorting requirement for residents is implemented.

Which one of the following statements logically follows from the information above?

(A) Most of the city's residents will continue to recycle even if a sorting requirement is implemented.

(B) If the city starts requiring residents to sort their recyclables, then all of the residents who continue to recycle will sort their recyclables.

(C) Implementing the sorting requirement would not cause the city's annual cost of sending garbage to its landfill to exceed its current annual cost of sorting recyclables.

(D) The amount of recyclables going to the city's landfill will increase if the sanitation department stays within its budget.

(E) If the city implements the sorting requirement, the sanitation department will stay within its budget.

22. Meerkat "sentinels," so-called because they watch for predators while other meerkat group members forage, almost never fall victim to those predators, yet the foragers often do. This advantage accruing to the sentinel does not mean that its watchful behavior is entirely self-interested. On the contrary, the sentinel's behavior is an example of animal behavior motivated at least in part by altruism. The loud bark emitted by the sentinel as it dashes for the cover of the nearest hole alerts other group members to the presence of danger.

Which one of the following is a questionable reasoning technique employed in the argument?

(A) appealing to evidence that tends to undermine rather than support the argument's conclusion

(B) appealing to evidence that presupposes the truth of the argument's conclusion

(C) inferring solely from an effect produced by an action that a purpose of the action is to produce that effect

(D) inferring solely from the claim that the behavior of a meerkat sentinel is not entirely selfish that this behavior is entirely altruistic

(E) concluding that a claim is false on the grounds that insufficient evidence has been offered to support it

23. Alex: Shrimp farming results in damage to the environment, because investors make quick profits from such farming and then abandon the farms.

Jolene: I disagree. Although some shrimp farms have proved unsustainable and have been quickly abandoned, properly built shrimp farms take a long time to construct and are costly to operate. Most owners try to make sure that their farms are productive for many years.

Their dialogue provides the most support for the claim that Alex and Jolene disagree with each other over whether

(A) most owners of shrimp farms eventually abandon their farms

(B) shrimp farming often yields a quick, easy profit

(C) shrimp farming hardly ever damages the environment

(D) abandonment of a shrimp farm results in damage to the environment

(E) some shrimp farmers are environmentally irresponsible

24. No one who works at Leila's Electronics has received both a poor performance evaluation and a raise. Lester has not received a raise, so it must be that he has received a poor performance evaluation.

The flawed reasoning in the argument above is most similar to the reasoning in which one of the following arguments?

(A) No one who lives in a house both owns it and pays rent on it. So, since my next-door neighbors pay rent on their house, it must be that they do not own it.

(B) No one who lives in a house both owns it and pays rent on it. My next-door neighbors own their house. Therefore, it must be that they do not pay rent on it.

(C) My neighbors have not paid any rent on their house. Since anyone who lives in a house but does not rent it owns it, it must be that they own it.

(D) My next-door neighbors do not own their house. Since no one who lives in a house both owns it and pays rent on it, it must be that my next-door neighbors pay rent on their house.

(E) Anyone who lives in a house but does not own it pays rent on it. My next-door neighbors do not own their house. Therefore, it must be that they pay rent on it.

GO ON TO THE NEXT PAGE.

25. Numerous studies have demonstrated a pronounced negative correlation between high-fiber diets and the incidence of colon cancer. For example, the colon cancer rate in Western countries is much higher than in many non-Western countries where people eat more fiber-rich foods, such as fruits and vegetables. Furthermore, in Scandinavia it has been conclusively shown that the higher the colon cancer rate in a given area, the lower the consumption in that area of cereals, which, like fruits and vegetables, are high in fiber. All of this shows that insufficient consumption of fiber causes colon cancer, and sufficient consumption of fiber prevents it.

The argument's reasoning is vulnerable to criticism because the argument overlooks the possibility that

(A) the consumption of fiber in many countries is rising appreciably

(B) the risk of many types of cancer is reduced by high-fiber diets

(C) fiber is difficult for many people to include in their diets

(D) the fiber in fruits and vegetables and the fiber in cereals have cancer-fighting properties to different degrees

(E) foods containing fiber also contain other substances that, when consumed, tend to prevent colon cancer

26. Anthropologist: Many people think that if human language evolved, then something like it must be present in those species most closely related to humans, such as chimpanzees. They reason that since new traits evolve gradually, something like human language, albeit cruder, must exist in some species from which humans evolved. This general line of argument may be reasonable, but it simply does not follow that chimpanzees have anything like human language, because humans did not evolve from chimpanzees. While chimpanzees are indeed closely related to humans, this is because both evolved from a common ancestor. The evolution of human language might easily have begun after the extinction of that common ancestor.

Which one of the following most accurately expresses the main conclusion of the anthropologist's argument?

(A) Humans did not evolve from chimpanzees, but rather from some extinct species.

(B) The assumption that something like human language must exist in some species from which humans evolved has no clearcut linguistic implications for chimpanzees.

(C) The communicative systems of chimpanzees are cruder than human language.

(D) Human language is a by-product of human intelligence, which chimpanzees lack.

(E) The evolution of human language began after the disappearance of an extinct species from which both humans and chimpanzees evolved.

S T O P
IF YOU FINISH BEFORE TIME IS CALLED, YOU MAY CHECK YOUR WORK ON THIS SECTION ONLY.
DO NOT WORK ON ANY OTHER SECTION IN THE TEST.

Topic Code	Print Your Full Name Here		
106133	Last	First	M.I.

Date	Sign Your Name Here
/ /	

Scratch Paper
Do not write your essay in this space.

LSAT® Writing Sample Topic

Directions: The scenario presented below describes two choices, either one of which can be supported on the basis of the information given. Your essay should consider both choices and argue for one over the other, based on the two specified criteria and the facts provided. There is no "right" or "wrong" choice: a reasonable argument can be made for either.

The Neeleys, a couple with two children ages eleven and thirteen, are planning a family vacation. They are deciding whether to drive their minivan to their vacation destination in the mountains or to fly there and back. The Neeleys have never vacationed in the mountains before. The vacation will last sixteen consecutive days. Using the facts below, write an essay in which you argue for one option over the other based on the following two criteria:

- The Neeleys want to spend as much time as possible engaged in physical recreational activities during their vacation.
- The Neeleys want to maximize the educational benefit the trip will have both for themselves and for their children.

Driving to the destination would take at minimum two and a half days each way. Delays—e.g., from road construction or mechanical breakdown—are more likely if the Neeleys drive than if they fly. The driving would be mostly across the vast interior plains and prairies of the country, which the children have never seen before. Often this geography is relatively featureless, with relatively few opportunities for activities such as swimming and hiking. Their route would take them near many historical sites and museums.

Flying to the destination and back would take about half a day each way, including the trip to the airport as well as security checks and waits. The children have never flown before. The mountains offer many opportunities for physical recreational activities. Even if they rent a car at their destination, few historical sites or museums would be within reach. The mountains exhibit a variety of geologically interesting rock formations and contain some archaeological sites.

WP-T10

Scratch Paper
Do not write your essay in this space.

LSAT Writing Sample Topic

LAST NAME (Print)

FIRST NAME (Print)

SSN/ SIN

L

MI

TEST CENTER NO.

SIGNATURE

M M D D Y Y
TEST DATE

LSAC ACCOUNT NO.

TOPIC CODE

Writing Sample Response Sheet

DO NOT WRITE
IN THIS SPACE

Begin your essay in the lined area below.
Continue on the back if you need more space.

COMPUTING YOUR SCORE

Directions:

1. Use the Answer Key on the next page to check your answers.

2. Use the Scoring Worksheet below to compute your raw score.

3. Use the Score Conversion Chart to convert your raw score into the 120–180 scale.

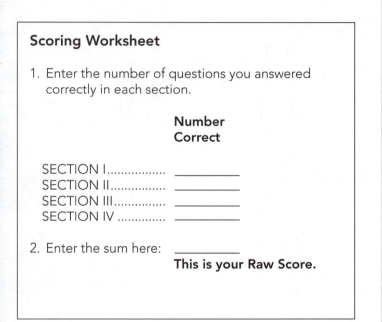

Scoring Worksheet

1. Enter the number of questions you answered correctly in each section.

	Number Correct
SECTION I.................	_____
SECTION II...............	_____
SECTION III..............	_____
SECTION IV	_____

2. Enter the sum here: _____
   This is your Raw Score.

Conversion Chart
For Converting Raw Score to the 120–180 LSAT Scaled Score
LSAT Form 3LSN100

Reported Score	Raw Score Lowest	Raw Score Highest
180	99	100
179	98	98
178	97	97
177	96	96
176	95	95
175	—*	—*
174	94	94
173	93	93
172	92	92
171	91	91
170	90	90
169	88	89
168	87	87
167	85	86
166	84	84
165	82	83
164	81	81
163	79	80
162	77	78
161	75	76
160	73	74
159	71	72
158	69	70
157	68	68
156	66	67
155	64	65
154	62	63
153	60	61
152	58	59
151	56	57
150	54	55
149	53	53
148	51	52
147	49	50
146	47	48
145	46	46
144	44	45
143	42	43
142	41	41
141	39	40
140	38	38
139	36	37
138	35	35
137	34	34
136	32	33
135	31	31
134	30	30
133	28	29
132	27	27
131	26	26
130	25	25
129	24	24
128	23	23
127	22	22
126	21	21
125	20	20
124	19	19
123	18	18
122	17	17
121	16	16
120	0	15

*There is no raw score that will produce this scaled score for this form.

ANSWER KEY

SECTION I

1.	E	8.	D	15.	E	22.	E
2.	D	9.	B	16.	B	23.	B
3.	A	10.	A	17.	B	24.	D
4.	B	11.	C	18.	D	25.	A
5.	A	12.	E	19.	C	26.	B
6.	C	13.	C	20.	A	27.	E
7.	B	14.	B	21.	D		

SECTION II

1.	E	8.	B	15.	E	22.	D
2.	D	9.	A	16.	A	23.	B
3.	D	10.	A	17.	C	24.	C
4.	B	11.	E	18.	A	25.	E
5.	C	12.	B	19.	D		
6.	E	13.	A	20.	D		
7.	D	14.	C	21.	A		

SECTION III

1.	E	8.	C	15.	A	22.	B
2.	E	9.	D	16.	D	23.	C
3.	B	10.	B	17.	*		
4.	A	11.	D	18.	A		
5.	C	12.	B	19.	C		
6.	E	13.	E	20.	A		
7.	A	14.	A	21.	C		

SECTION IV

1.	A	8.	D	15.	B	22.	C
2.	C	9.	A	16.	C	23.	B
3.	E	10.	A	17.	E	24.	D
4.	B	11.	B	18.	E	25.	E
5.	B	12.	A	19.	D	26.	B
6.	C	13.	D	20.	D		
7.	B	14.	E	21.	D		

*Item removed from scoring.